Back Stitch, Ringed

In this stitch, Back Stitches are worked in a formation to produce half-rings. A second row of stitches completes the rings.

The connecting stitches between the rings are worked into the same holes.

All stitches must be firmly pulled.

In the detail opposite, Stranded Cotton colour 0204 is used to work the Ringed Back Stitches and the Four-Sided Stitch. At the edges, Eyelet Holes in Stranded Cotton colour 0205 can be seen. Four-Sided Stitch is on page 52 and Eyelet Holes on page 42.

Fig 1 Bring the thread through at A, insert it at B (2 threads down) and bring it out at C (4 threads up and 2 threads to the left).

Fig 2 Insert the needle at A (2 threads down and 2 threads to the right) and bring it out at D (2 threads up and 4 threads to the left).

Fig 3 Insert the needle at C (2 threads to the right), and bring it out at E (2 threads down and 4 threads to the left).

Fig 4 Insert the needle at D (2 threads up and 2 threads to the right) and bring it out at F (4 threads down and 2 threads to the left), to complete a half-ring.

Fig 5 Continue working half-rings as shown.

Fig 6 Turn the fabric round and work Figs 1–5 to complete the rings.

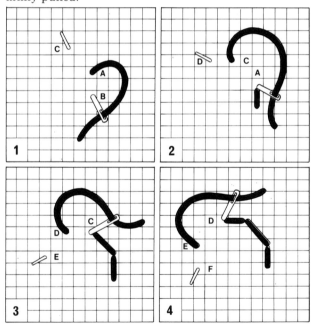

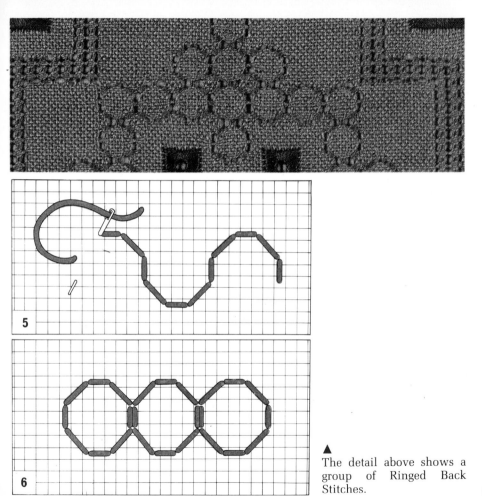

▲
The detail above shows a group of Ringed Back Stitches.

5

Back Stitch: Whipped Back Stitch

The ship motif opposite is worked in Back Stitch, Whipped Back Stitch, Cross Stitch and Straight Stitch. Stranded Cotton colour 0403 is used with 2 strands in the needle.

Fig 1 Bring the needle through at A, insert the needle at B (two threads to the right), and bring out at C (4 threads to the left).

Fig 2 Insert the needle at A (2 threads to the right).

Fig 3 Bring the needle out at D (4 threads to the left).

Fig 4 Insert the needle at C (2 threads to the right), and bring it out at E (2 threads down and 4 threads to the left).

Fig 5 Insert the needle at D (2 threads up and 2 threads to the right) and bring it out at F (4 threads down and 2 threads to the left).

Continue in this way following the line of the

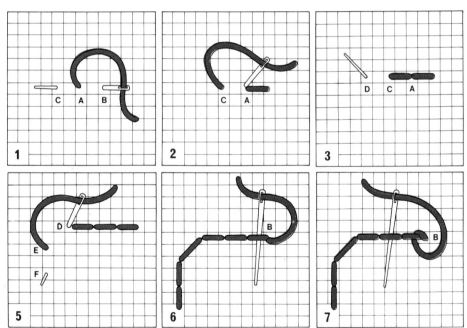

6

design to the last stitch.

Whipped Back Stitch
Fig 6 With another thread in the needle, bring the thread through at B, pass the needle under the first stitch already made, without piercing the fabric.

Fig 7 Pass the needle under the next stitch without piercing the fabric.

Fig 8 The finished effect of Back Stitch with Whipping worked over the stitches.

Ship in Blackwork
The ship motif is a Black-work embroidery where there is a high contrast between the colour of the embroidery thread and the ground fabric. Blackwork was a popular decoration in the sixteenth century and coloured threads, dark blue, brown, green and red, were sometimes used, together with metallic threads.

Ship (approximate size 11 × 12.5cm)▼

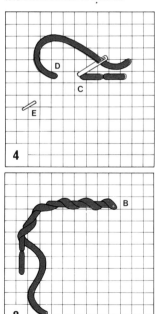

Cable Stitch

This stitch can be worked over any even number of fabric threads. In the design opposite, stitches are worked over 4 fabric threads, and this is demonstrated in the diagrams.

Stranded Cotton colours 0890, 0901, 0264, 0266 and 0268 are used.

Fig 1 Bring the thread through at A and insert the needle at B (4 threads to the right) and bring it out at C (1 thread down and 2 threads to the left).

Fig 2 Insert the needle at D (4 threads to the right) and bring it out at B (1 thread up and 2 threads to the left).

Fig 3 Insert the needle at E (4 threads to the right) and bring it out at D (1 thread down and 2 threads to the left).

Fig 4 Insert the needle at F (4 threads to the right) and bring it out at E (1 thread up and 2 threads to the left). Continue working in this way.

The Band design opposite would look effective worked on a set of place mats with, perhaps, a section of the border worked round matching napkin rings.

The design is also suitable for rectangular cloths, such as tray cloths, trolley cloths and bureau runners, or could be worked on a drum-shaped fabric lampshade, to co-ordinate with cushions banded with the design.

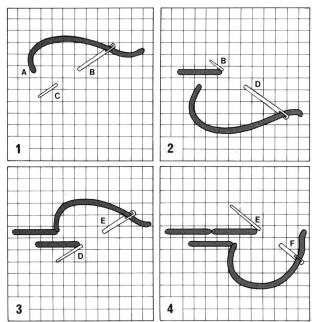

Band ▶

A working chart for the design is on page 100.

Chequer Filling

This stitch is formed by first working diagonal rows of Oblong Cross Stitches, then a second Oblong Cross Stitch is superimposed. Stitches are firmly pulled as they are worked and this produces the attractive open effect which can be seen in the detail.

In this, Chequer Filling is worked in massed rows to produce an area of texture and is also worked in single rows. Fig 1 shows the first stage of working and Fig 2 the second stage.

Diamond Eyelets (page 32) also form part of the design.

Fig 1 Bring the thread through at A and insert the needle at B (6 threads up and 2 threads to the left) and bring the needle out at C (2 threads down and 2 threads to the left), Continue making Oblong Cross Stitches as shown, C–D, D–E, E–F, F–G, then complete the Oblong Cross Stitch as shown, G–D, D–E, E–B, B–C, C–H.

To work the superimposed Cross Stitches, bring the thread out at I (6 threads to the left).

Insert the needle at J (2 threads up and 6 threads to the right) and bring it out at K (2 threads up and 2 threads to the left).

Continue working in this way to the end of the row.

Fig 2 This shows the completed stitch in the first row and half the stitch worked in the second row, with the needle in position to complete the superimposed Cross.

10 **1**

Chequer Filling is one of the stitches used in pulled thread or pulled fabric work where the stitch binds the fabric's warp and weft threads to produce holes which form a pattern.

Traditionally, pulled thread work used fabric and thread of the same colour but attractive effects are achieved with subtle colour combinations, or with contrasting threads and fabrics.

The detail opposite shows the effect of Chequer Filling Stitch worked in Stranded Cotton colours 0361 and 0362.

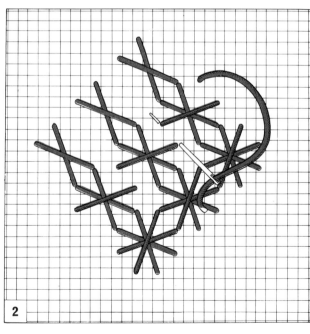

2

Chessboard Filling

This stitch consists of triple rows of Satin Stitches making horizontal and vertical rectangular blocks. The diagram shows blocks worked with 10 Satin Stitches, over 3 fabric threads commencing at A. All stitches must be firmly pulled to achieve the open effect.

Chessboard

The design opposite has Chessboard Filling Stitch in the central area, worked in white Stranded Cotton. The decorative border in Four-sided Stitch uses colour 086, with Satin Stitch blocks in the same colour.

This pretty motif can be used singly or as a repeat for a border, or, for an all-over effect, set motifs so that the edges are joined. The resulting design would look very effective for a cushion or would make a large, central area for a tablecloth.

For a different effect, Double Knot Stitch (page 40) could be used for the areas outlining the Filling, or another Filling could replace Chessboard. Cobbler Filling (page 16) or perhaps a block of Greek Cross Stitch Lacy Filling (page 56) could be worked. Many of the Filling stitches can be interchanged in designs, thus providing an almost endless source of inspiration.

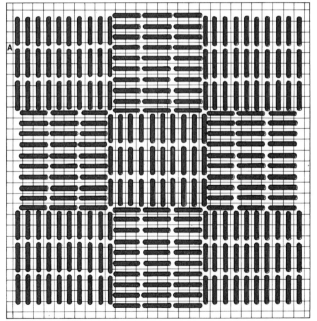

Chessboard ▶
A working chart for the design is on page 101.

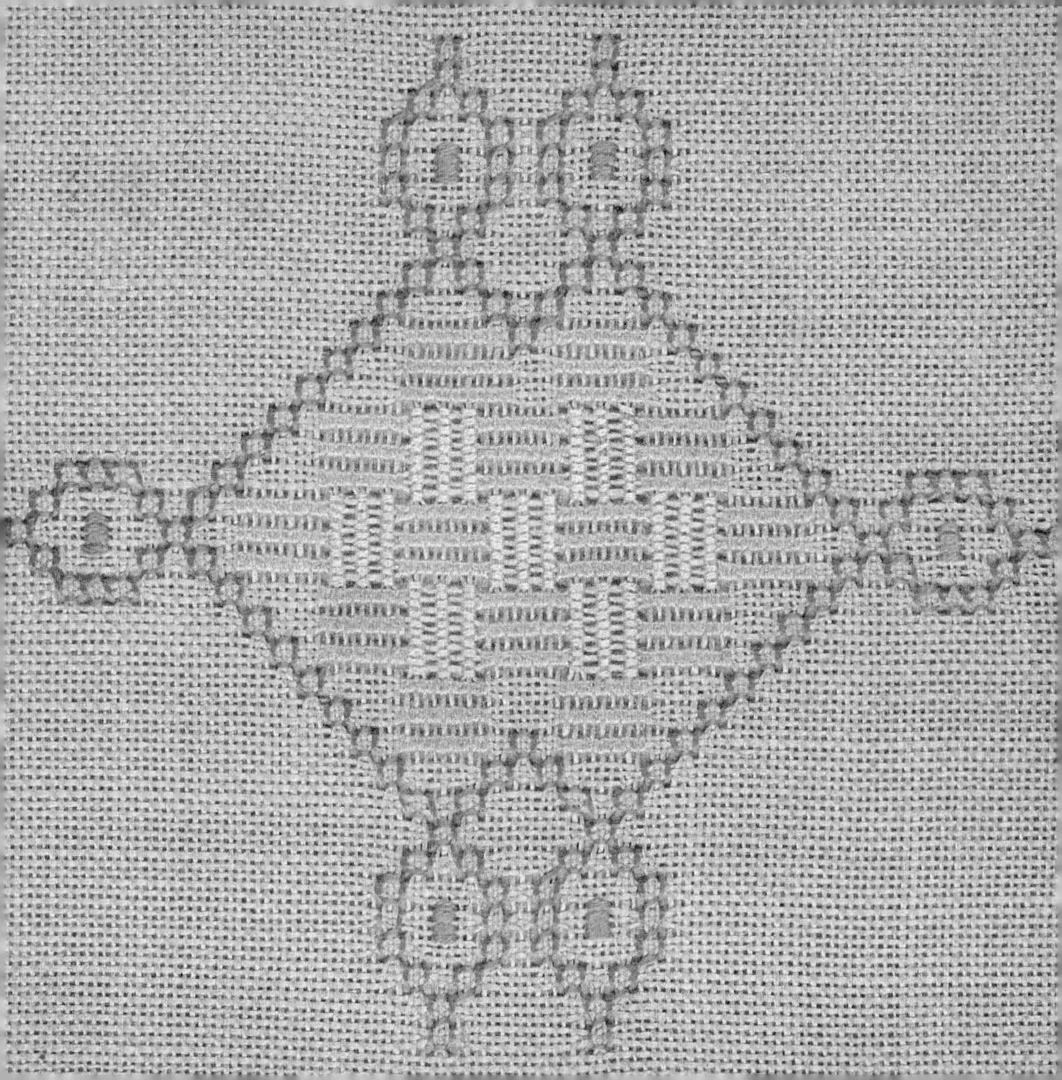

Chevron Stitch

This filling stitch may be worked over any number of threads. A chart for the design opposite is on page 102.

Fig 1 Bring the thread through at A, insert the needle at B (4 threads to the right), and bring it out at C (2 threads to the left).

Fig 2 Insert the needle at D (4 threads up and 2 threads to the right) and bring it out at E (2 threads to the left).

Fig 3 Insert the needle at F (4 threads to the right) and bring it out again at D (2 threads to the left).

Fig 4 Insert the needle at G (4 threads down and 2 threads to the right) and bring out at B (2 threads to the left).

Fig 5 Insert the needle at H (4 threads to the right) and bring it out again at G (2 threads to the left).

Fig 6 Insert the needle at I (4 threads up and 2 threads to the right) and bring it out at F (2 threads to the left). Continue in sequence.

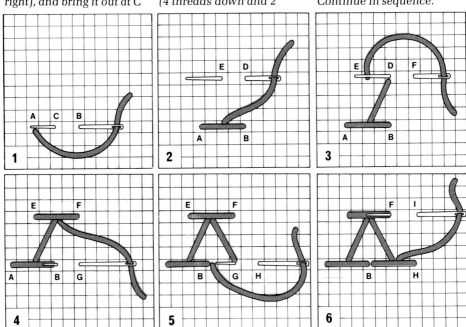

14

Cobbler Filling

This stitch consists of Straight Stitches worked over 4 threads of fabric and alternately spaced, leaving 2 and 4 threads between stitches. Stitches should be pulled firmly to achieve the open effect.

Whipped Back Stitch (page 6) has been used with the Cobbler Filling, using Pearl Cotton Nos 5 and 8.

Fig 1 Work all the vertical stitches first in rows. Bring the thread through at A, insert the needle at B, bring it out at C and insert it at D. Continue working in this way.

Fig 2 Work the horizontal stitches in rows in the spaces between the vertical stitches, to form squares. Bring the thread through at E, insert the needle at F, bring it out at H and insert it at G. Continue working in this way.

Cobbler

The detail on the opposite page shows an area of Cobbler Filling. This Filling can be used on many of the designs in this book, where fillings are part of the design. It could, for instance be worked in the central motif of the Abbess design on pages 18–19 as an alternative to Coil Filling.

Designs such as Square on Square on page 59 could be used for Cobbler Filling. A single motif might be set at the ends of a tray cloth or used on a larger item, such as a tablecloth.

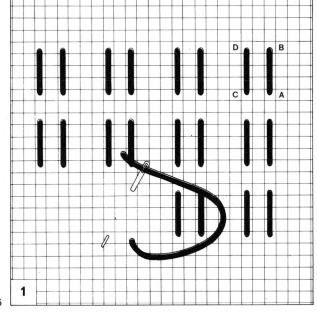

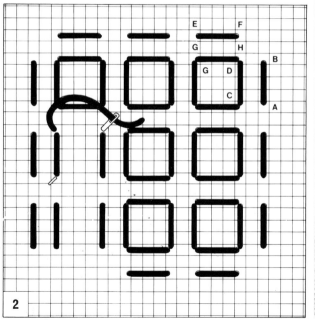

This detail shows Cobbler
Filling Stitch, set into a
decorative shape, outlined
with Whipped Back Stitch
▶

Coil Filling

This stitch consists of clusters of three Satin Stitches being worked in the same place, with an even number of fabric threads between each cluster.

When working Coil Filling, all stitches must be firmly pulled.

Working the Filling

Commence at A (see diagram) and at the end of each row make a small stitch into the back of the last cluster to secure the working thread before commencing the next row.

Abbess Motif

The design opposite has an area of Coil Filling Stitch in the centre of the design, providing interesting tex-

tural contrast with the Back Stitched and Satin Stitched areas. The same design, Abbess, is shown on pages 88–89 with an alternative filling stitch, demonstrating the versatility of these stitches and the different kinds of effects that can be achieved.

The embroidery is worked in white Pearl Cotton 5 and 8.

This type of design is ideal for a variety of home linens and furnishings. Its soft, flowing lines would look well set as a main motif on place mats, with perhaps the corner Crosses set on a matching napkin.

Linked with rows of Crosses, the motifs could be positioned at the corners of a large tablecloth, or might make an effective design for a bed coverlet.

The Cross and Scroll section of the design could be abstracted for a border repeat on a set of huckaback guest towels.

Abbess ▶

A working chart for the design is on page 103.

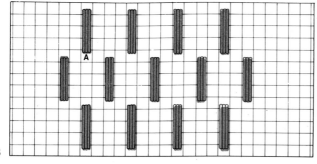

Cretan Stitch

This stitch can be worked over any number of threads, to form a close stitch or an open pattern.

In the design opposite, an open stitch is worked over varying numbers of threads in the central, orange area, the rows worked in yellow thread are a regular open stitch, while the rows worked in gold coloured thread on the edges of the border are worked in a close stitch. Rows of Satin Stitch are also used in this border design.

Fig 1 Bring the thread through at A, insert the needle at B (6 threads up and 2 threads to the right) and bring it out at C (4 threads down), the thread under the needle point.

Fig 2 Insert the needle at D (6 threads down and 2 threads to the right) and bring it out at E (4 threads up) keeping the thread under the needle point.

Fig 3 Insert the needle at F (6 threads up and 2 threads to the right) and bring it out at G (4 threads down) keeping the thread under the needle point.

Fig 4 Insert the needle at H (6 threads down and 2 threads to the right) and bring it out at I (4 threads up) keeping the thread under the needle point. Continue working in sequence.

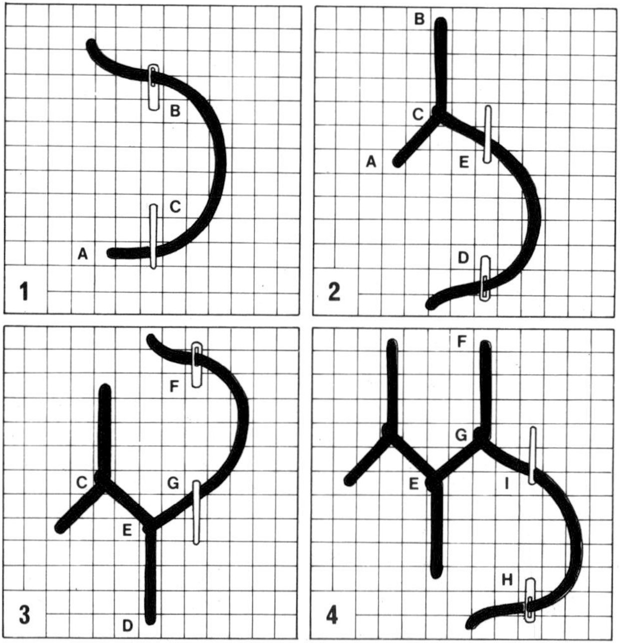

Border ▶

A working chart for the design is on page 104.

20

Cross Stitch

Cross Stitch may be worked from right to left or left to right and the upper stitch of the Cross can slope in either direction. However, it must lie in the same direction throughout. A working chart for the design is on page 105.

Fig 1 Bring the thread through at A, insert it at B (2 threads up and 2 threads to the left) and bring it out at C (2 threads down).

Fig 2 Insert the needle at D (2 threads up and 2 threads to the left) and bring it out at E (2 threads down).

Fig 3 Continue as shown.

Fig 4 To complete the upper half of the Cross, bring the thread through at I (2 threads down), insert the needle at F (2 threads up and 2 threads to the right), and bring it out at G (2 threads down).

Fig 5 Continue to complete the Crosses.

Fig 6 The finished effect.

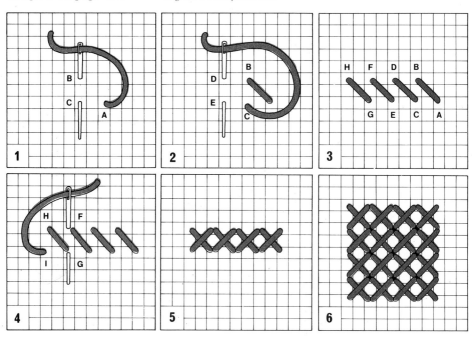

Diagonal Raised Band and Filling

This stitch consists of Crosses worked diagonally across the fabric, each stitch being firmly pulled to achieve an open effect.

Fig 1 Bring the thread through at A, insert the needle at B (4 threads up) and bring it out at C (2 threads down and 2 threads to the left).

Fig 2 Insert the needle at D (4 threads up) and bring it out at E (2 threads down and 2 threads to the left). Continue working in this way.

Fig 3 After completing the last stitch at H, bring the needle through at I (2 threads down and 2 threads to the left) insert the needle at F (4 threads to the right) and bring it out at G (2 threads down and 2 threads to the left) in readiness for the next stitch.

Fig 4 This shows the completed row of Cross Stitches.

Fig 5 Rows of Cross Stitches worked closely together.

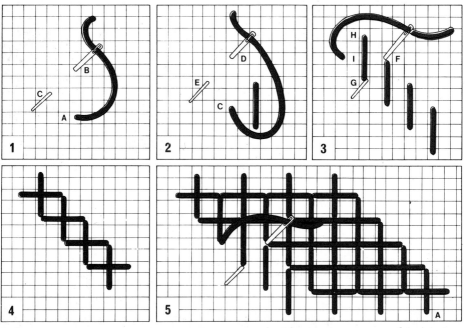

Diagonal Raised Band Filling: Open Trellis

This is another variation on the Diagonal Raised Band Filling stitch. Each Cross is worked over 6 threads of fabric.

Fig 1 *Commence at A and work rows of Diagonal Raised Bands (refer to page 24 for working instructions), spacing the rows as shown on this page.*

Fig 2 *To create the Trellis pattern, commence at B and work rows of Diagonal Raised Bands in the opposite direction, to cross the previous rows of stitches at regular intervals.*

Note that the method of working the crosses in Fig 2 differs from those shown in Fig 1, the horizontal stitches being worked first, followed by the vertical stitches. Where the rows intersect, a heavier cross is formed by the double stitches.

This stitch should be firmly pulled to achieve the open effect.

Open Trellis

The detail opposite is from an embroidery worked in two different threads for contrast. Stranded Cotton colour 0398 is used for the Filling, and colour 0399 for the Diamond Eyelets (see page 32). The Satin Stitch border is worked with Pearl Cotton No. 5, colour 0399.

The working instructions for Satin Stitch can be found on page 86.

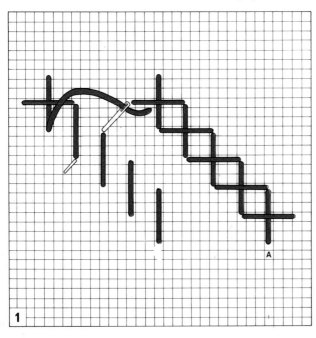

1

The detail right shows an example of Diagonal Raised Band Filling, with Diamond Eyelets and a border of Satin Stitches. ▶

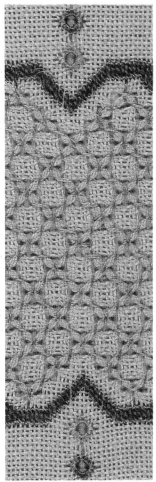

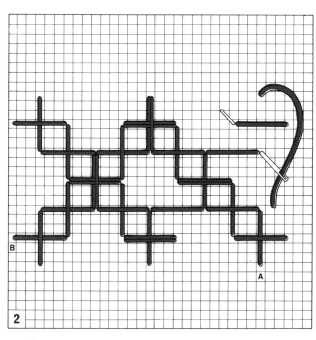

2

Diagonal Raised Band Filling: Variation

In this variation, each Cross is worked over 6 fabric threads and the rows of Crosses are spaced (see diagram). Follow the stage by stage instructions on page 24 for working the stitch, working stitches over 6 threads.

Stitches should be pulled firmly to achieve the open effect.

Eight-point Star

The Star design opposite is worked in Stranded Cotton in two closely toned colours, 0870 for the filling and 0871 for the Satin Stitch central diamond and the outer border.

Diagonal Raised Band Filling Variation produces an interesting texture which can be utilised in a variety of embroidery projects. The formal motif, opposite, illustrates one way; that of containing the texture within a geometric shape. The Filling could also be worked in Satin Stitch-edged bands to make borders for designs for household linens or for fashion accessories. For instance, alternate rows of Diagonal Raised Band Filling Variation and Satin Stitch could be worked across an elegant purse, with the Variation worked on a matching wide belt.

Eight-point Star ▶

A working chart for the design is on page 106.

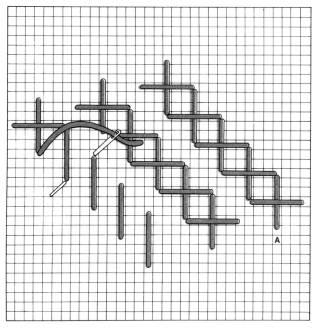

Diagonal Satin Filling

This stitch consists of blocks of Satin Stitches worked diagonally. The design opposite shows that the stitch can be used as a border design or can be set into geometric shapes.

Working the Filling

Commence at A and work the first block. Work the second block, vertically or horizontally, with the Satin Stitches slanting in the opposite direction. (See diagram.)

For a different effect, the Satin Stitches can be worked in the same direction throughout. Stitches must be firmly pulled to achieve the effect.

Snowflake

The design opposite is worked in one colour, Stranded Cotton colour 0120, but this motif could also be worked using two or more colours for a different effect.

The main motif, within the border can be developed into a continuous border design and used on items such as curtains or on tie-backs.

Five motifs, worked in a cross formation could become the central design on a large tablecloth.

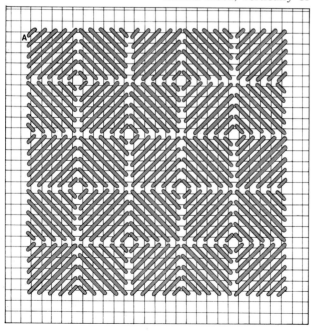

Snowflake ▶

A working chart for the design is on page 107.

Diamond Eyelet

This stitch forms a diamond shape worked over an even number of horizontal and vertical fabric threads. In the design opposite the largest Eyelet is worked over 28 threads, the middle-sized over 20 threads and the smallest over 12 threads. Fern Stitch, Back Stitch and Satin Stitch are also used in this pretty border design.

In diagrams 1–5, Diamond Eyelet is worked over 10 vertical and 10 horizontal fabric threads.

Fig 1 Bring the needle through at A, insert it at B (5 threads down) and bring it out again at C (4 threads up and 1 thread to the left).

Fig 2 Insert the needle again at B (4 threads down and 1 to the right) and bring it out at D (3 threads up and 2 threads to the left).

Fig 3 Insert the needle at B (3 threads down and 2 threads to the right) and bring it out at E (2 threads up and 3 threads to the left).

Fig 4 Insert the needle at B (2 threads down and 3 threads to the right) and bring out at F (1 thread up and 4 threads to the left).

Fig 5 Continue working in this sequence to complete a Diamond Eyelet.

Mountain Flowers ▶

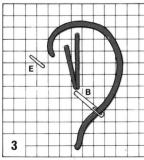

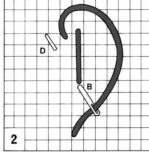

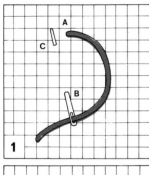

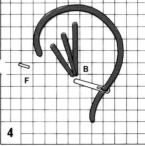

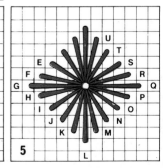

32

Diamond Filling

This consists of Double Back Stitches worked in stepped lines to make zigzag rows. Two zigzag rows are worked to form a diamond pattern (see diagram).

Refer to pages 36–37 for Double Back Stitch.

Working the stitch

Commence at A and work over the same number of fabric threads throughout. The broken lines indicate the direction of the connecting thread between stitches on the reverse side.

The size and shape of the 'diamonds' can be varied by lengthening or shortening the zigzag lines.

Stitches should be firmly pulled for an open effect.

The design opposite is worked using white Pearl Cotton, and would look effective on a traycloth or table cloth. A working chart for the Diamond Filling design is on page 109.

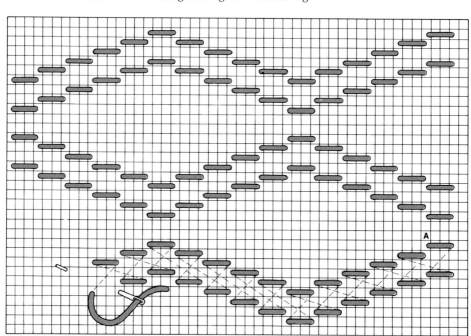

Double Back Stitch: Finnish Filling

The attractive border design opposite is worked with diagonal stepped lines of Double Back Stitches, producing Finnish Filling.

Fig 1 Bring the thread through at A and insert the needle at B (2 threads to the right) and bring it out at C (4 threads down and 2 threads to the left).

Fig 2 Insert the needle at D (2 threads to the right) and bring it out at E (4 threads up and 4 threads to the left).

Fig 3 Insert the needle at A (2 threads to the right) and bring it out at F (4 threads down and 2 threads to the left and level with C).

Fig 4 Insert the needle at C and bring it out at G. Continue in this way.

Fig 5 This shows the finished effect.

Finnish Filling
This consists of blocks of Double Back Stitches worked from right to left in diagonal stepped lines to form an all-over filling (see detail opposite).

Fig 6 Commence at A and work over the same number of threads throughout. The broken lines indicate the direction of the connecting thread between stitches on the reverse side. The first row of blocks of stitches are shown in grey. The second row is shown in colour.

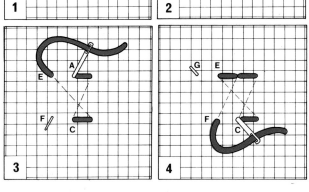

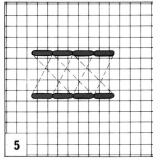

36

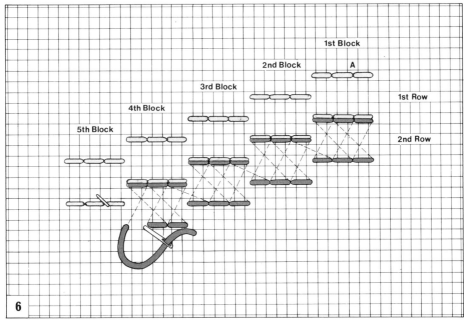

1st Block

2nd Block

A

3rd Block

1st Row

4th Block

2nd Row

5th Block

6

Double Cross Stitch

The pretty abstract flower motif opposite is worked with Double Cross Stitch, Back Stitch and Whipped Back Stitch, using Stranded Cotton in a range of pastel colours, 0110, 0109, 0108, 075, 076, 0900 and 8581.

The Spring Flower motif is designed so that it can form a border along a tray cloth or trolley cloth, or it might make a pretty individual motif on a small accessory, such as an oven glove.

Fig 1 Bring the thread through at A, insert it at B (4 threads up and 4 threads to the left), and bring it out at C (4 threads down).

Fig 2 Insert the needle at D (4 threads up and 4 threads to the right) and bring it out at E (4 threads down and 2 threads to the left).

Fig 3 Insert the needle at F (4 threads up) and bring it out at G (2 threads down and 2 threads to the left).

Fig 4 Insert the needle at H (4 threads to the right) and bring it out at C (2 threads down and 4 threads to the left) in readiness to commence the next stitch.

Fig 5 This shows a group of Double Cross Stitches. The last upper stitches of each Cross should lie in the same direction.

Spring Flower ▶
A working chart for the design is on pages 110–111.

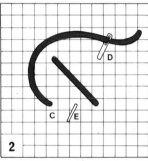

1

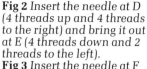

2

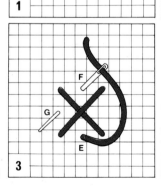

3

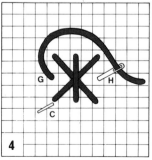

4

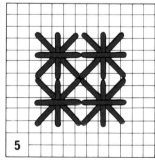

5

38

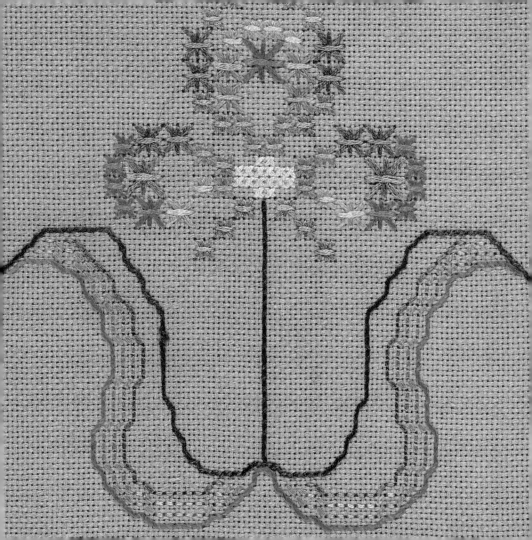

Double Knot Stitch

This stitch has been used in the design opposite to form a fairly heavy, textured line, contrasting with the lighter lines of Back Stitches. Cross Stitches are also used in the embroidery to form stylised flower motifs at the centre.

The design could be adapted to make a kind of 'meander' border for house linens.

Stranded Cotton is used to work the design, colours 066, 068, 0109 and 0110.

Fig 1 Bring the thread through at A, insert it at B (2 threads down and 1 thread to the right) and bring it out at C (2 threads to the left).

Fig 2 Pass the needle behind the stitch just made without piercing the fabric.

Fig 3 Pull the thread through and pass the needle behind the lower half of the stitch without piercing the fabric and keeping the thread under the needle point. Pull the thread through to form a knot.

Fig 4 Insert the needle at D (2 threads down from B) and bring it out at E (2 threads to the left) in readiness for the next stitch.

Fig 5 This shows the finished effect of Double Knot Stitch.

Maze ▶

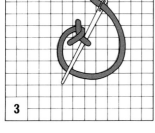

1

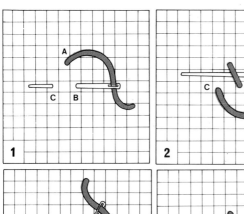

3

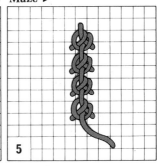

2

4

5

40

Eyelet Holes

This stitch forms a square over an even number of vertical and horizontal threads of fabric.

The design opposite, made up of Eyelet Holes in four different sizes, is worked in Stranded Cotton, colours 01, 0390, 0391, 0392 and 0926. Satin Stitch is also used in the design.

In Figs 1–6, an Eyelet Hole is demonstrated working over 6 vertical and 6 horizontal threads of fabric.

Fig 1 *Bring the thread through at A and insert it at B (3 threads down and 3 threads to the left). Bring it out at C (3 threads up and 2 threads to the right).*

Fig 2 *Insert the needle again at B (3 threads down and 2 threads to the left) and bring it out at D (3 threads up and 1 thread to the right).*

Fig 3 *Insert the needle again at B (3 threads down and 1 thread to the left) and bring it out at E (3 threads up).*

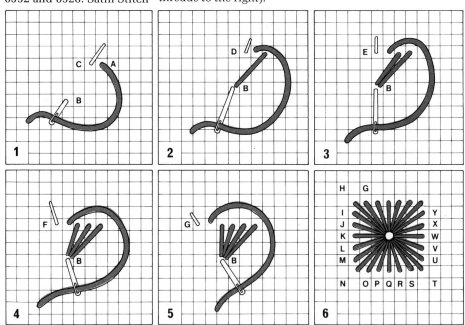

42

Fig 4 *Insert the needle again at B (3 threads down) and bring it out at F (3 threads up and 1 thread to the left).*

Fig 5 *Insert the needle again at B (3 threads down and 1 thread to the right) and bring it out at G (3 threads up and 2 threads to the left).*

Fig 6 *Continue working in sequence to complete the Eyelet Hole.*

Geometric

The design can be adapted to form new designs, by grouping the four sizes of Eyelets in other ways. Eyelets can be linked with linear stitches, such as Back Stitch or Double Knot Stitch.

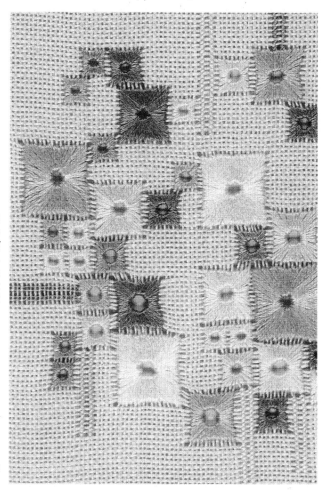

Geometric ▶

A working chart for the design is on page 112.

Double Faggot Filling

This stitch is used for the textured square areas in the design opposite and Satin Stitches are used to form the border of the design. Stranded Cotton colour 0968 is used to work the embroidery.

Fig 1 Bring the thread through at A and insert the needle at B (4 threads to the right) and bring it through again at A.

Fig 2 Re-insert the needle at B and bring it through at C (4 threads down and 4 threads to the left).

Fig 3 Insert the needle at A (4 threads up) and bring it through again at C.

Fig 4 Re-insert the needle at A and bring it through at D (4 threads down and 4 threads to the left).

Fig 5 Continue in this way following the alphabetical sequence to the end of the row. Complete the last stitch, G–F, by re-inserting the needle in F and bringing it out at H (4 threads down and 4 threads to the

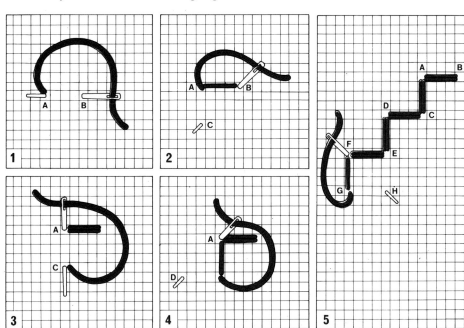

44

right). Turn the work round to work the last row.

Fig 6 *Bring the thread through at H and insert the needle at G and bring it through again at H.*

Continue working in the same way as the previous row. Stitches must be firmly pulled in working to achieve the open effect.

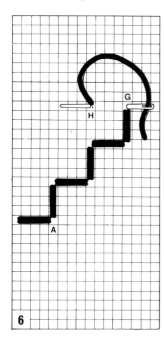

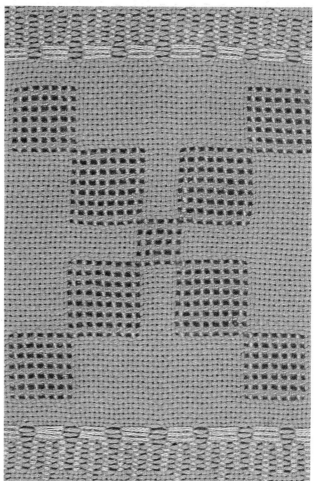

Reversed Faggot Filling

This kind of Filling where threads are pulled firmly to produce an open texture, contrasts well with stitches such as Satin and Back Stitch. It is illustrated in the detail opposite.

Fig 1 Bring the thread through at A, insert the needle at B (4 threads down and 4 threads to the right) and bring it out at C (4 threads to the left).

Fig 2 Insert the needle at D (4 threads down and 4 threads to the right) and bring it out at B (4 threads up).

Fig 3 Insert the needle at E (4 threads down and 4 threads to the right) and bring it out at D (4 threads to the left).

Fig 4 Insert the needle at F (4 threads down and 4 threads to the right) and bring it out at G (4 threads down), in position to commence the next row.

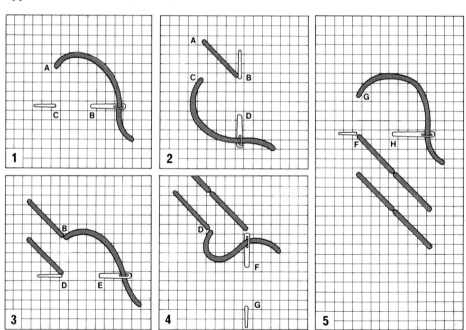

46

To work the next and following rows, turn the fabric round and continue working in the same way.

Fig 5 Insert the needle at H (4 threads down and 4 threads to the right) and bring it out at F (4 threads to the left).

Fig 6 Re-insert the needle at D (4 threads down and 4 threads to the right) and bring it out at H (4 threads up).

Fig 7 Continue working in sequence where the connecting stitches between the rows are worked into the same holes.

All stitches must be firmly pulled.

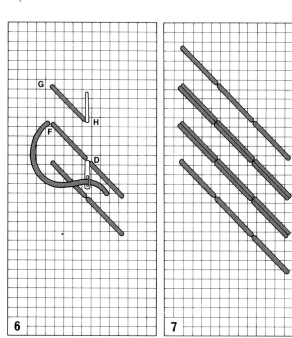

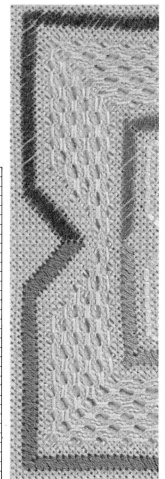

47

Fern Stitch

This stitch consists of three Straight Stitches radiating from the same central point. Stitches can be worked over any number of fabric threads. The charming motif opposite uses Fern Stitch for the 'tree', with Back Stitch, Satin Stitch and Cross Stitches making up the design. Stranded Cotton, colours 01, 046 and 0244 has been used.

Fig 1 Bring the thread through at A, insert it at B (4 threads up) and bring it out at C (4 threads to the left).

Fig 2 Insert the needle again at A (4 threads down and 4 to the right), and bring it out at D (4 threads up and 4 threads to the right).

Fig 3 Insert the needle again at A (4 threads down and 4 to the left) and bring it out at E (4 threads down).

Fig 4 Insert the needle again at A (4 threads up) and bring it out at F (4 threads to the left). Continue working in sequence.

Fig 5 This shows the finished effect of Fern Stitch.

Festive Tree ▶
A working chart for the design is on page 113.

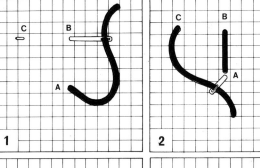

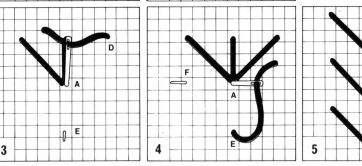

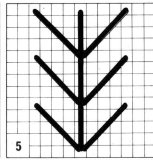

48

Fly Stitch

This versatile stitch can be worked over any number of threads to produce different decorative effects. The design opposite is worked entirely in Fly Stitch. Stranded Cotton, colour 034, has been used for the embroidery.

Fig 1 Bring the thread through at A, hold the thread down with the thumb, insert the needle at B (4 threads to the right) and bring it out at C (2 threads down and 2 threads to the left), with the thread under the needle point.

Fig 2 Insert the needle at D (2 threads down) to complete the stitch.

Fig 3 This shows a single Fly Stitch.

Fig 4 Fly Stitches can also be worked in rows, as on the border of the design opposite.

Fig 5 Stitches can also be set vertically.

The motif of four 'crosses' could be set at the corners of a table cloth or on one corner of a tray cloth. Individual crosses could also be worked across the end of a tray cloth or runner, or would look effective set as a border for a table cloth, with a row of Fly Stitches worked along the hem.

Four-cross ▶
A working chart for the design is on page 114

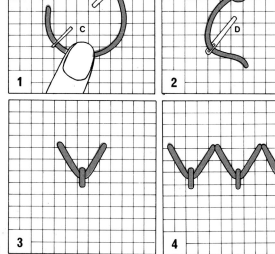

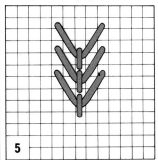

50

Four-sided Stitch

This stitch produces a close, textural effect.

Fig 1 Bring the thread through at A, insert it at B (4 threads up) and bring it out at C (4 threads down and 4 threads to the left).

Fig 2 Insert the needle at A (4 threads to the right) and bring it out at D (4 threads up and 4 threads to the left).

Fig 3 Insert the needle at B (4 threads to the right) and bring it out at C (4 threads down and 4 threads to the left).

Fig 4 Work a Straight Stitch from C–D.

Fig 5 Alternatively, continue working as shown. To work a second row, turn the fabric and work stitches in the same way, the connecting stitches between the blocks being worked into the same holes.

Flower corner ▶
A working chart for the design is on page 115.

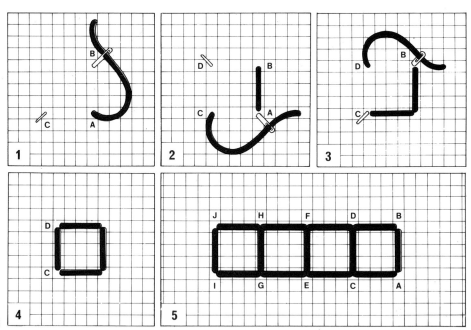

Four-sided Stitch: Variation

In this variation horizontal rows of Four-sided Stitches are worked over four vertical and four horizontal fabric threads. Each alternate row begins with half a Four-sided Stitch (see diagram), so that the stitches lie evenly spaced between the stitches of the row above.

Refer to page 52 for the instructions for working Four-sided Stitch. Stitches must be firmly pulled.

Maltese Cross

The design opposite uses the Four-sided Stitch variation for the 'Maltese Cross' motif, with Satin Stitch and Eyelet Holes at the corner areas. Stranded Cotton, colour 0942, has been used throughout the embroidery.

The motif is ideal for setting at the corners of a square table cloth or trolley cloth but could also be used in conjunction with a drawn thread border. The 'Maltese Cross' area of the design, with its open texture would make a suitable border design for an embroidered lampshade.

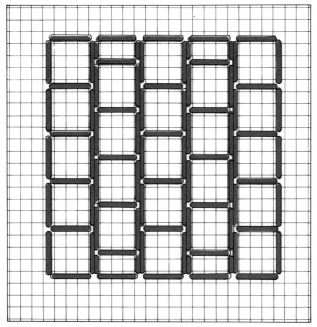

Maltese Cross ▶
A working chart for the design is on page 116.

54

Greek Cross Stitch: Lacy Filling

The Filling consists of diagonal rows of Greek Cross Stitches. The stitch is best worked in a frame.

Fig 1 Bring the thread through at A, insert the needle at B (4 threads up and 4 threads to the right), and bring it through at C (4 threads down), keeping the thread under the needle point.

Fig 2 Pull the thread through and insert the needle at D (4 threads to the right) and bring it through again at C (4 threads to the left) in the exact position

shown in the diagram, keeping the thread under the needle point.

Fig 3 Pull the thread through and insert the needle at E (4 threads down) and bring it through again at C (4 threads up), keeping the thread under the needle point.

Fig 4 Pull the thread through and secure the Cross, insert the needle again at C, overlapping the last and first stitches.

Fig 5 Greek Cross Stitch.

Lacy Filling
To work the Filling, commence the first stitch at A (see diagram right) and work over the same number of threads throughout. The broken lines indicate the

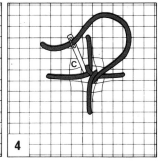

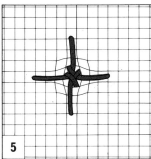

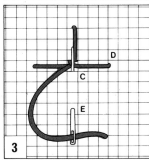

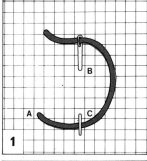

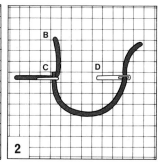

direction of the connecting thread between stitches, on the reverse side.

Completing the first row, work the second diagonal row in the same direction and subsequent rows in the same way. All stitches must be firmly pulled.

The detail shows an example of Greek Cross Stitch Lacy Filling.

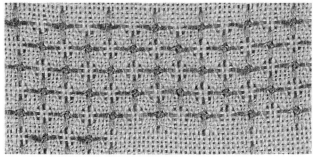

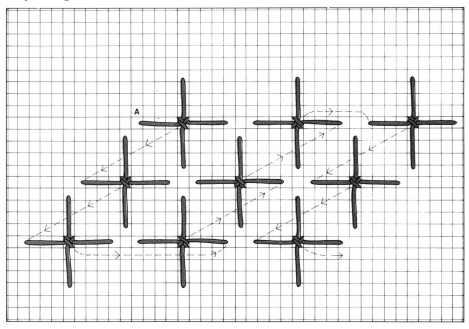

Greek Cross Stitch: Squared Filling

This stitch consists of Greek Cross Stitches worked in diagonal rows, set so that the Crosses make a square formation.

Stitches must be firmly pulled to achieve the required open effect.

Working the stitch

Following the diagram, commence the first stitch at A and work over the same number of fabric threads throughout. The broken lines indicate the direction of the connecting thread between stitches, on the reverse side.

On completion of the first diagonal row, turn the fabric and work the next diagonal row in the same direction as the first. Work subsequent rows in the same way.

The design is worked in Stranded Cotton colour 06 and Pearl Cotton 06.

Square on Square ▶

A working chart for the design is on page 117.

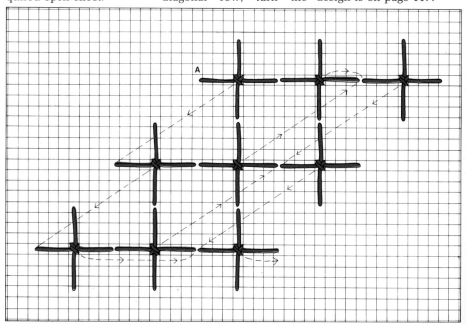

Hedebo Buttonhole Stitch: Edging with Picot

The fabric edge is folded back to the wrong side, to approximately twice the depth of the Hedebo Buttonhole Stitch. The stitch is then worked over the folded edge through both thicknesses of fabric.

Fig 1 Bring the thread through at A, on the fold between the two layers of fabric and insert the needle at B at the back of the work (3 threads down and 1 thread to the right).

Fig 2 Pull the needle through leaving a loop of thread, then pass the needle through the loop and pull upwards to form a stitch.

Fig 3 Insert the needle at C from the back of the work (3 threads down and 1 thread to the right) in readiness for the next stitch.

Fig 4 This shows the finished effect of the stitch. To turn a corner, three or four stitches are worked into the same hole as shown, then continue.

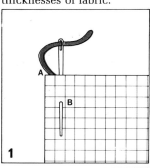

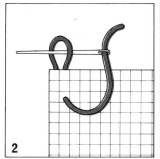

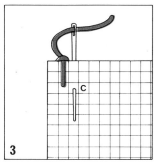

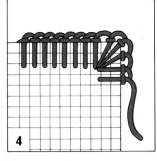

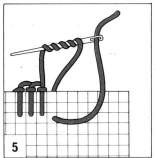

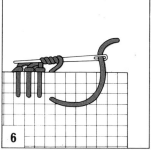

Edging with Picot

Fig 5 Begin by working a few Buttonhole Stitches (Figs 1 to 3), then instead of passing the needle through the loop, encircle the needle with the thread as shown. The more twists of thread the larger the picot.

Fig 6 To keep the picot in position, tighten the working thread and pull the thread through.

Fig 7 To secure the picot, pass the needle behind and through the looped edge of the previous stitch.

Fig 8 Insert the needle from the back of the work for the next stitch.

Fig 9 The finished effect.

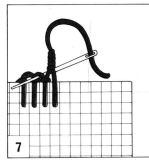

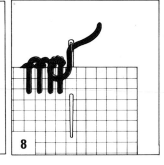

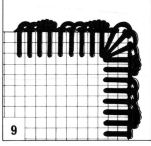

Hemstitch: Diamond Hemstitch

To work this stitch, threads are withdrawn on each side of a solid fabric area. The design opposite shows rows of the stitch worked over 3 withdrawn threads, 6 threads of fabric left, 3 withdrawn threads.

Fig 1 Bring the thread through at A and insert the needle at B (4 threads to the right), and pass the needle and thread from B to A behind 4 loose fabric threads.

Fig 2 Pull the stitch firmly and insert the needle at C (3 threads up) and bring it out at D (4 threads to the left).

Fig 3 Pull the thread through and re-insert the needle at C (4 threads to the right) and bring it out again at D.

Fig 4 Pull the stitch firmly and insert the needle at E (3 threads down) and bring it out at F (4 loose threads to the left).

Fig 5 Re-insert the needle at E (4 loose threads to the right) and bring it out again at F.

Continue in this way to the end of the row.

Fig 6 Turn the work round and work the second row in the same way with the connecting stitches worked into the same central holes of the first row.

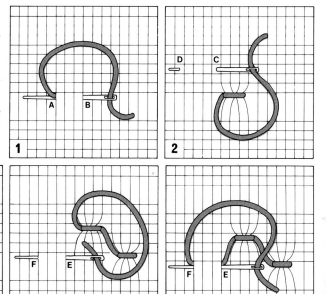

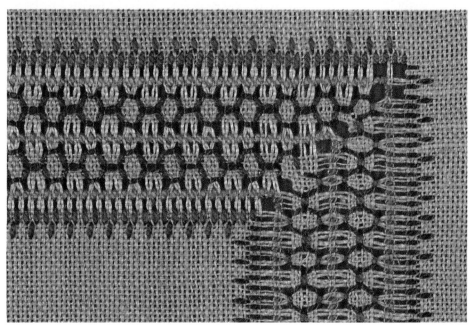

The border design above uses two other stitches, Satin Stitch and Straight Stitch, both worked in Pearl Cotton No. 5, colours 0373 and 0375.

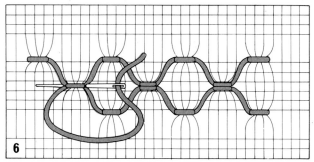

6

Hemstitch: Interlaced

To work this stitch, withdraw the required number of fabric threads across the fabric. Work Hemstitch (refer to page 66), along both edges of the space of drawn threads to create Ladder Hemstitch. Then proceed as follows:

Fig 1 *Fasten a long thread centrally at A at the right side of the loose threads. Pass the needle across the front of two pairs of threads and pass the needle from left to right behind pair B and over pair C.*

Fig 2 *Keeping the needle and thread on the upper surface, and in one movement, twist pair B over pair C by passing the needle from right to left behind pair C.*

Pull the interlacing thread through firmly to lie in position through the centre of the twisted pairs of threads.

Star Band

In the design opposite, Interlacing has been worked using 6mm (¼in)-wide satin ribbon, to provide textural interest to the embroidery. Stranded Cotton, colour 049 and Pearl Cotton, colour 02 are used for the Satin Stitched bands while the central, decorative pattern of star shapes is worked in Satin Stitches and Fly Stitches.

Decorative bands such as this have a wide variety of uses in embroidery for the home and for fashion. The band is ideal for edging rectangular cloths and runners or it could be worked down one, or both, sides of a place mat. Half of the pattern, including the central decorative area, could be worked round a lampshade, and the design lends itself to an all-over embroidery for a cushion. The band could be worked round both ends of a matching bolster for a co-ordinated furnishing scheme.

In fashion applications, the design might be worked across a soft purse or shoulder bag, along a wide belt, or, worked on fairly coarsely woven evenweave dress fabric, the band would look effective bordering a skirt or on sleeve ends.

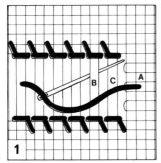

1

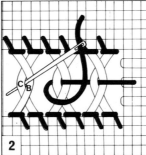

2

64

Star Band ▶
A working chart for the design is on page 119.

Hemstitch: Ladder Hemstitch

Fig 1 Bring the needle through at A. Pass the needle and thread from B to C behind 2 loose vertical fabric threads (2 threads up and 2 loose threads to the left).

Fig 2 Pull the thread through and re-insert the needle at B (2 loose threads to the right) and bring it out at D (2 threads down and 2 threads to the left). Pull firmly.

Fig 3 This shows the effect of Hemstitches.

Fig 4 To work Ladder Hemstitch, work Hemstitch along both edges of the drawn thread space. To create the ladder effect, take care to work corresponding pairs of loose threads on opposite sides of the drawn thread space.

Flower Border

The pretty border on the opposite page has two areas of Ladder Hemstitching with Hemstitch Interlacing set between Satin Stitch stylised flower motifs worked in.

The design is ideal for bordering a variety of house linens.

Stranded Cotton, colour 0388 is used for the Ladder Hemstitches, with Pearl Cotton, colours 0259, 0261 and 0388 for the remainder of the embroidery.

To prepare the fabric, withdraw the required number of fabric threads.

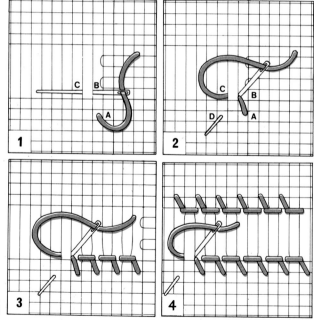

Flower Border ▶

A working chart for the flower motif is on page 120.

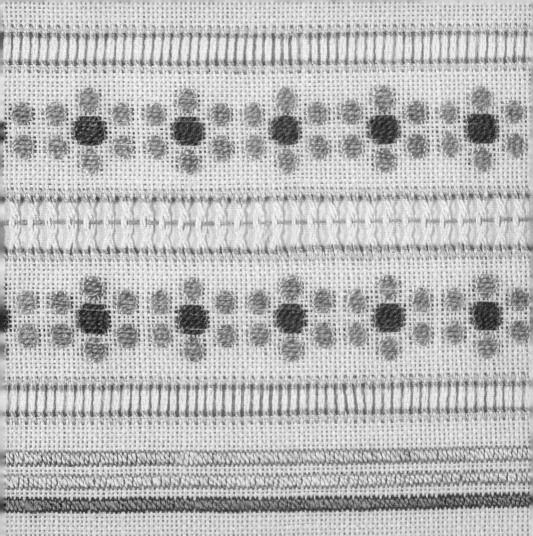

Hemstitch: Zigzag

This is a popular stitch used in drawn thread embroidery, and is used to good effect in the border opposite, where it is combined with Four-sided Stitch and Satin Stitch for textural contrast.

Stranded Cotton, colours 01 and 0939 are used on pale blue fabric, producing a fresh, pretty effect.

Working the stitch

To work the stitch, withdraw the required number of fabric threads (the diagram shows 4 threads withdrawn). Work Hemstitch along one edge of the space of drawn threads (refer to page 62 for working instructions), but make sure that there is an even number of threads in each group of loose threads caught together. (The diagram shows 2 threads in each group but in the design opposite, 4 threads are caught together in each group.)

On the opposite edge, work Hemstitches as shown in the diagram, dividing the groups of fabric threads equally. A half group starts and ends the second row.

White and Blue

To work the design opposite as follows from the outside edge: two rows of Four-sided Stitch are worked over 4 threads each, leave 8 threads, withdraw 8 threads for Zigzag Hemstitching, leave 12 threads and work one row of Four-sided Stitch down the centre, withdraw 8 threads for Zigzag Hemstitching, leave 8 threads and finish the border on the inside edge with 2 rows of Four-sided Stitch each worked over 4 threads.

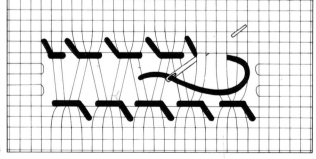

White and Blue ▶

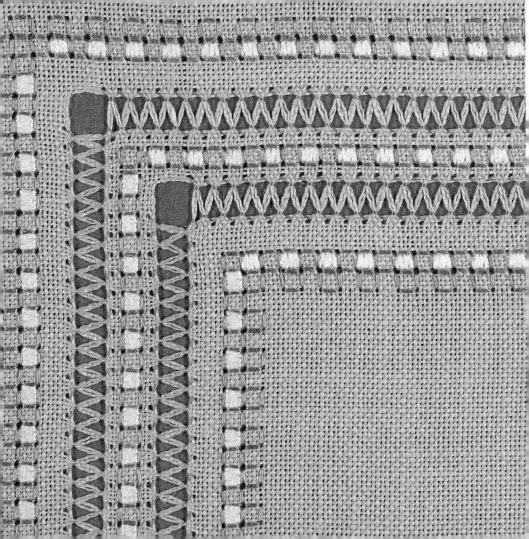

Herringbone Stitch

This stitch can be worked over any number of fabric threads.

Fig 1 Bring the thread through at A, insert the needle at B (2 threads down and 2 threads to the right) and bring it out at C (2 threads to the left).

Fig 2 Insert the needle at D (4 threads up and 4 threads to the right) and bring it out at E (2 threads to the left).

Fig 3 Insert the needle at F (4 threads down and 4 threads to the right) and bring it out at G (2 threads to the left).

Fig 4 Insert the needle at H (4 threads up and 4 threads to the right) and bring it out at I (2 threads to the left).

Fig 5 Insert the needle at J (4 threads down and 4 threads to the right) and bring it out at K (2 threads to the left).

The design opposite is worked in Stranded Cotton, colours 0875, 0886, 0888 and 0906.

Cross Stitches are used with Herringbone Stitches in the design and, if desired, could be used to extend the design for a corner motif, or as part of a border.

Herringbone motif ►
A working chart for the design is on page 121.

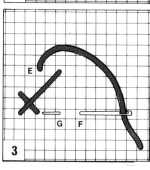

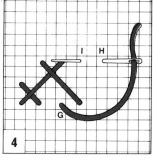

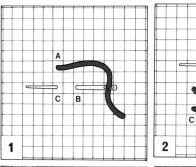

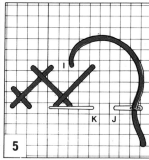

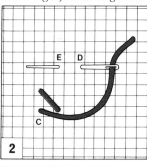

Holbein Stitch

This is also known as Double Running Stitch. An even line of embroidery is achieved by first working a row of Running Stitches, then a second row is worked, the needle being inserted at one side of the worked stitch and coming out on the other side.

Fig 1 Bring the thread through at A and insert the needle at B (2 threads to the left) and bring it out at C (2 threads down).

Fig 2 Insert the needle at D (2 threads to the left) and bring it out at E (2 threads down).

Fig 3 Continue in this way, following the line of the design to the last stitch.

Insert the needle at X and bring it out again at W (2 threads to the right).

Fig 4 Re-insert the needle at Y and bring it out at Z. Continue in this way, filling the spaces between the stitches of the first row.

Holbein ▶

A working chart for the design is on page 122.

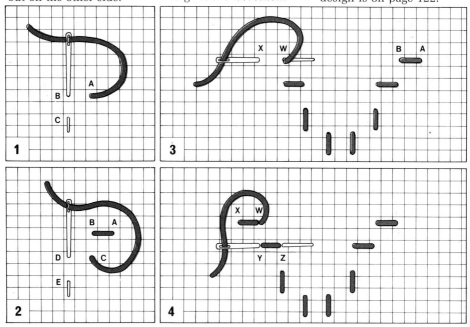

Honeycomb Filling

This textured Filling stitch is used for the central cross in the design.

Fig 1 Bring the thread through at A, insert the needle at B (2 threads to the right) and bring it out at C (2 threads down).

Fig 2 Insert the needle again at B (2 threads up) and bring it out again at C (2 threads down).

Fig 3 Insert the needle at D (2 threads to the left) and bring it out at E (2 threads down).

Fig 4 Insert the needle again at D (2 threads up) and bring it out again at E (2 threads down).

Fig 5 Continue as shown.

Fig 6 To work a second row, work stitches as Figs 1 to 4. The connecting stitches between the rows are worked into the same holes. Stitches must be firmly pulled to achieve the desired effect.

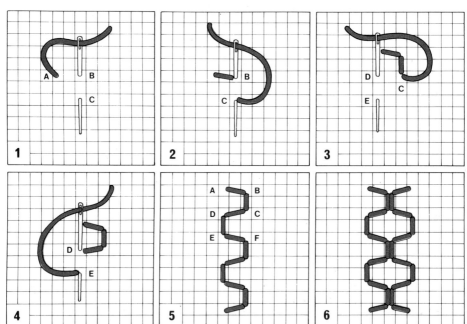

Mosaic Filling

Stitches must be firmly pulled to achieve the open effect of this Filling.

Fig 1 Starting at A, work 5 Satin Stitches over 3 fabric threads, to form a block. On completion of the last Satin Stitch, bring the needle through again at B in posi-tion to work the next block.

Fig 2 Work 4 blocks of Satin Stitches to form a square. On completion of the last stitch, bring the needle through at D.

Fig 3 Work a Four-sided Stitch (refer to page 52), and on completion, bring the needle through again at D.

Fig 4 Insert the needle at B (4 threads up and 4 threads to the left) and bring it out at C (4 threads down) to work a Half Cross Stitch.

Fig 5 Insert the needle at A (4 threads up and 4 threads to the right) to complete the Cross Stitch.

Fig 6 Mosaic Filling.

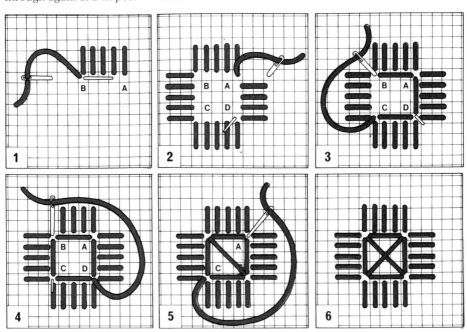

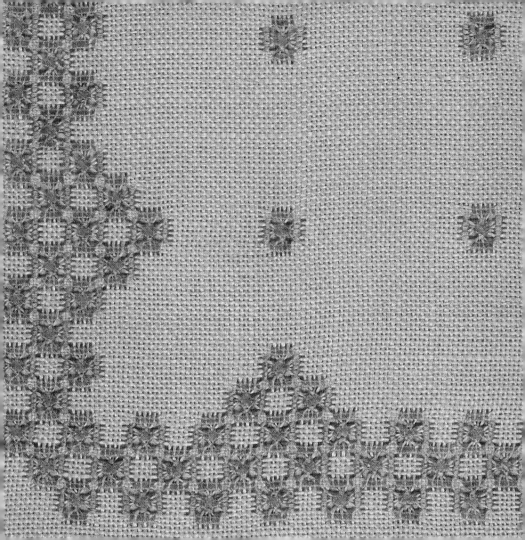

Needleweaving

Needleweaving is worked over the loose threads left after withdrawing fabric threads. This border consists of blocks of weaving which are worked diagonally across the loose threads using different embroidery thread colours, and interconnecting to form attractive patterns. The diagrams, Figs 1 to 6, illustrate the basic working method for all needleweaving, with the connecting stitch worked over and under the loose threads common to both blocks, forming the link between each block.

Pearl Cotton No. 5, colours 0264, 0267, 0268, 0301 and 0338 are used in the design opposite and this could be worked as decorative bands on the ends of a runner.

Fig 1 Bring the thread through at A, insert the needle at B (over 4 loose threads to the right), pass the needle behind the loose threads and bring it out again at A.

Fig 2 Insert the needle at C (over 4 loose threads to the

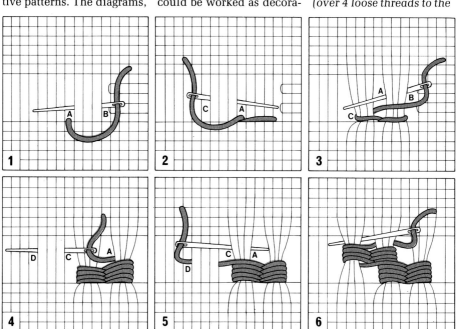

left), pass the needle behind the loose threads and bring it out at A.

Fig 3 Insert the needle at B (over 4 loose threads to the right), pass the needle behind the loose threads and bring it out at A.

Continue working in this way for the required depth.

Fig 4 To work the connecting block, bring the thread through at A, insert the needle at C (over 4 loose threads to the left) and bring it out at D (behind 4 loose threads to the left).

Fig 5 Insert the needle at C (over 4 loose threads to the right) and bring it out at A (behind 4 loose threads to the right).

Fig 6 Continue working stitches in this way.

Needleweaving ▼

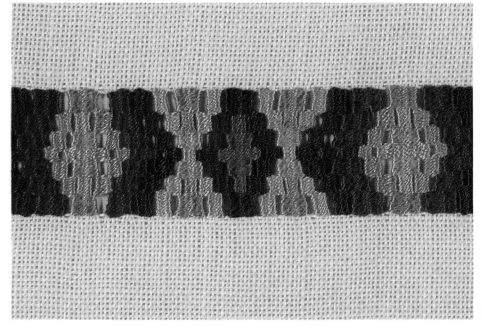

Outlined Diamond Eyelet Filling

This filling consists of Diamond Eyelets worked over an even number of vertical and horizonal threads with Diagonal Satin Stitches outlining the Eyelet (see diagram). In the diagram, the Eyelet is worked over 12 fabric threads, with the Diagonal Satin Stitches worked over 2 intersections.

All stitches are firmly pulled to achieve the effect.

In the design opposite, the outlined Eyelets are worked over 14 horizontal and 14 vertical threads. The Eyelets and Diagonal Satin Stitch are worked in Stranded Cotton colour 0969, with the Whipped Back Stitch motifs in colour 0970.

Spanish motif ▶
A working chart for the design is on page 123.

Punch Stitch

This stitch has been used for the 'leaves' of the stylised flower motif opposite. Pull all stitches firmly.

Fig 1 Bring the thread through at A, insert it at B (4 threads up) and bring it out again at A; insert the needle again at B and bring it out at C (4 threads down and 4 threads to the left).

Fig 2 Insert the needle at D (4 threads up) and bring it out again at C.

Fig 3 Insert the needle again at D and bring it out at E (4 threads down and 4 to the left) in readiness for the next stitch. Continue working in this way for the required length.

Fig 4 Turn the fabric to work the next and following, rows. Work stitches in the same way as Figs 1 to 3.

Fig 5 To complete the squares, turn the fabric sideways and work stitches as before.

Fig 6 The finished stitch.

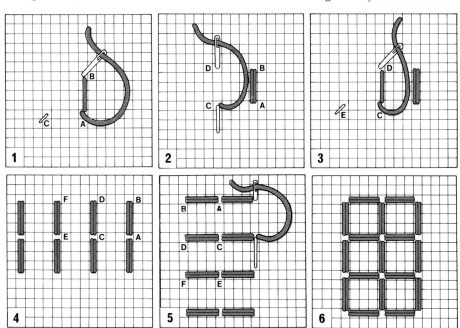

Ripple Filling

This Filling consists of blocks of Double Back Stitches worked in rows from right to left in alternate blocks of Double Back Stitches and spaces (see diagram).

Refer to page 36 for the instructions for working Double Back Stitch.

Working the stitch

Commence the first block of the first row at A and work over the same number of fabric threads throughout. Work the following rows, spacing as shown in the diagram, to form an all-over filling.

The broken lines indicate the direction of the connecting thread between the stitches and the blocks on the reverse side. The grey stitches indicate the first row of blocks, while the coloured stitches indicate the second and third rows of blocks.

Stitches should be firmly pulled to achieve an open effect.

This Filling is best worked in a frame.

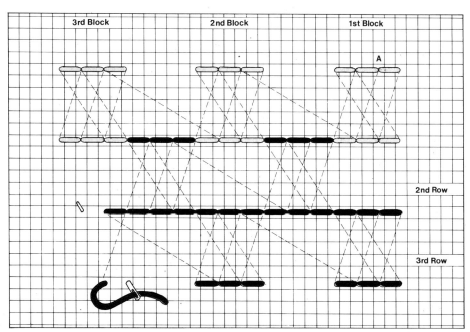

Satin Stitch

This stitch can be worked vertically, horizontally, or diagonally over varying numbers of fabric threads.

The pretty design opposite, worked in subtle shades of pink and green, combines Satin Stitch, Cross Stitch, Back Stitch and Star Stitches.

Fig 1 To work vertical Satin Stitch, bring the thread through at A and insert the needle at B (6 threads up) and bring it out at C (6 threads down and 1 to the right).

Fig 2 Insert the needle at D (6 threads up) and bring it out at E (6 threads down and 1 to the right).

Continue working

stitches in this way.

Fig 3 This shows Satin Stitch being worked horizontally.

Fig 4 This shows Satin Stitch being worked diagonally.

Flower Garden

The design, worked as a square, could be adapted to make a border, looking a little like a row of flowers. One half of the square motif, taken diagonally, could be used as an attractive corner design, set on a square or rectangular place mat or trolley cloth.

Stranded Cotton, colours 06, 08, 024, 052, 0854, 0856 and 0887 have been used to work the design.

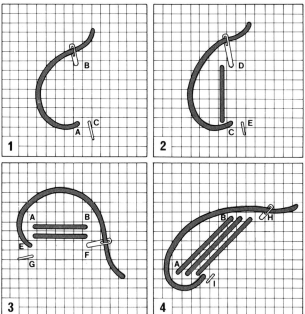

Flower Garden ▶

Spaced Satin Filling

This stich consists of blocks of Satin Stitches evenly spaced across the fabric. Stitches must be firmly pulled to achieve the open effect.

Working the stitch

Commence at A and work the first row of blocks, working vertically or horizontally. The second row of blocks is worked so that they are positioned between the blocks of the first row.

Continue working rows of blocks to fill the desired space.

White on white

The attractive white-on-white design on the opposite page is the Abbess motif, also shown on page 19. It would make an elegant border, repeated on the hems of curtains or on square or rectangular cloths. The design can also be used as a single element, or the two motifs that make up the design could be used singly, or repeated to make borders.

Whipped Back Stitch and Satin Stitch are also used in the design, worked in white Pearl Cotton Nos. 5 and 8.

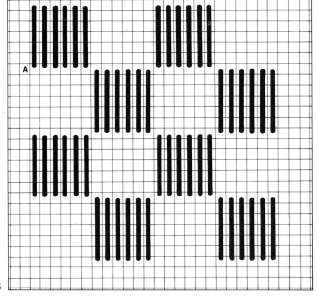

A working chart for the Abbess design is on page 103.

Squared Edging Stitch

This stitch is used to finish fabric edges and consists of two rows of stitchery. Begin at the left side of the work, leaving sufficient fabric to turn back a hem.

Working from top to bottom, work the first row of stitches on all the edges and corners (Figs 1–4) before turning the hem.

Fig 1 Bring the thread through at A, insert the needle at B (3 threads to the right) and bring it out at C (3 threads down and 3 threads to the left).

Fig 2 Insert the needle at A (3 threads up) and bring it out again at C (3 threads down).

Fig 3 Insert the needle at D (3 threads to the right) and bring it out at E (3 threads down and 3 threads to the left). Continue working this sequence for the required length of edging.

Fig 4 To turn the corner, after completing the stitch K to L, bring the needle

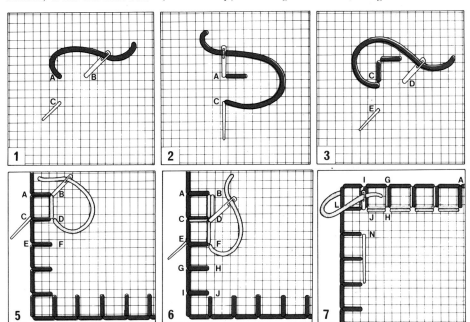

through at J (3 threads up), insert it again at L (3 threads down) and bring it out at M (3 threads to the right). Insert the needle again at L (3 threads to the left) and bring it out at M (3 threads to the right). Turn the work and continue working the edges, and corners in this way.

Turning the hem

On completion of the first row of stitchery, turn back the fabric at the edge, level with the outer vertical stitch, to form a hem.

The second row of stitchery (shown as grey in the diagrams Figs 5–8) is worked through both layers of fabric.

Fig 5 *Bring the thread through at D, insert the needle at B (3 threads up), bring the needle back through at D (3 threads down) and insert again at B (3 threads up), then pass the needle diagonally behind the work and bring it round at C.*

Fig 6 *Insert the needle at D (3 threads to the right) and bring it out at F (3 threads down). Re-insert the needle at D (3 threads up), bring it out again at F (3 threads down). Re-insert the needle again at D and bring it round at E. Continue working in this sequence to within 4 vertical stitches of the corner.*

Fold back the surplus fabric at the lower edge to form a corner (4 layers of fabric). Insert the needle at D (3 threads up), through

all layers of fabric, then pass the needle diagonally behind the work and bring it round at E. Continue working in this way to the corner, finishing with a Straight Stitch from I to J.

Fig 7 *To turn the corner, turn the work. Pass the needle behind the work and bring it round at L, insert the needle at J (3 threads to the right) and bring it out at N (3 threads down).*

Fig 8 *Continue working the remaining edges and corners in the same way. On completion carefully trim away surplus fabric on the wrong side of the work, close to the double line of stitching.*

The detail above shows an example of Squared Edging Stitch.

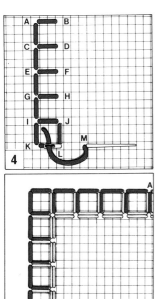

Star Stitch

This stitch forms a square over an even number of horizontal and vertical fabric threads. In the design opposite, the Stars are worked over 12 and 6 threads of fabric.

The diagrams, Figs 1 to 5, show the stitch worked over 4 threads.

In the design opposite Stranded Cotton colours 0310, 0328 and 0330 are used for the embroidery.

Fig 1 Bring the thread through at A and insert the needle at B (2 threads down and 2 threads to the left) and bring it out at C (2 threads up).

Fig 2 Insert the needle again at B (2 threads down) and bring it out at D (2 threads up and 2 threads to the left).

Fig 3 Insert the needle again at B (2 threads down and 2 threads to the right) and bring it out at E (2 threads to the left).

Fig 4 Insert the needle again at B (2 threads to the right) and bring it out at F (2 threads down and 2 threads to the left).

Fig 5 Continue working in sequence to complete the Star Stitch.

Stars ▶

A working chart for the design is on page 125.

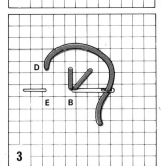

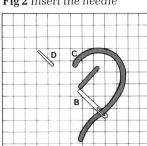

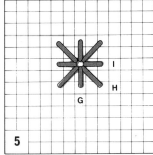

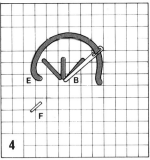

Step Filling

This stitch consists of blocks of vertical and horizontal Satin Stitches lying at right angles to each other, evenly spaced.

Working the stitch

Commence at A and work each row of blocks diagonally. All the stitches must be firmly pulled to achieve the effect of the Filling, shown in the central textured area of the design opposite.

Five Cross

The design would make an ideal central motif for a small cloth or could be set at the corners of a larger cloth with a border of Satin Stitches worked in Pearl Cotton.

Stranded Cotton colour 0336 has been used for the stitch, with colour 4146 for the centres of the Satin Stitched crosses. The crosses are worked in Pearl Cotton No. 5, colour 0778.

The Filling could also be extended in area to fill the four quarters of the cross, with perhaps an unworked band of fabric diagonally bisecting the area.

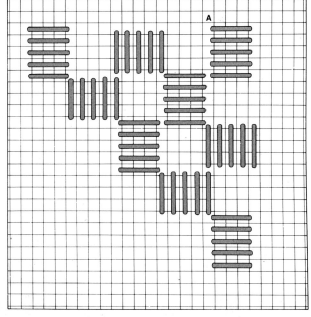

Five-cross ▶
A working chart for the design is on page 126.

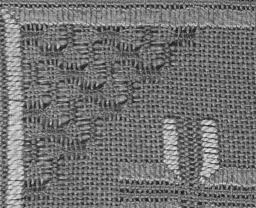

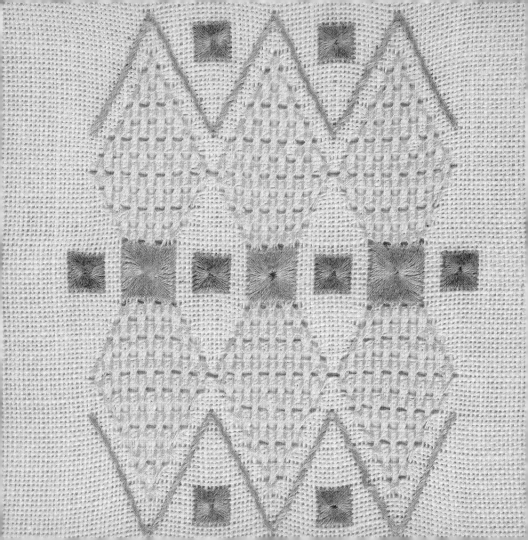

Wave Stitch

Diagonal Straight Stitches are worked in horizontal rows and firmly pulled.

Fig 1 Bring the thread out at A, insert the needle at B (4 threads up and 2 threads to the right) and bring it through at C (4 threads to the left).

Fig 2 Insert the needle at A (4 threads down and 2 threads to the right) and bring it out at D (4 threads to the left).

Fig 3 Insert the needle at C (4 threads up and 2 to the right) and bring it out at E (4 threads to the left).

Fig 4 Insert the needle at D (4 threads down and 2 threads to the right) and bring it out at F (4 threads to the left).

Fig 5 To work the second row, complete the stitch F to E and bring the thread out at G (8 threads down) insert the needle at F (4 threads up and 2 threads to the left) and bring it out at D (4 threads to the right).

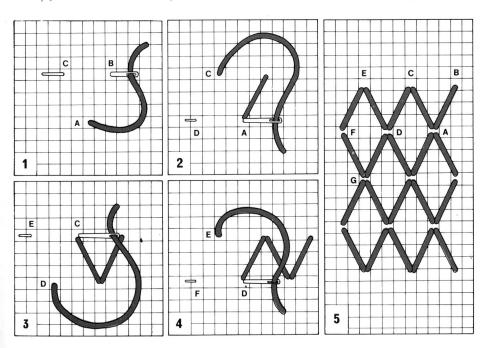

Working with Counted Thread

Charts

The colour pictures on previous pages show the effect of the finished stitch and ways in which it can be combined with other stitches to create attractive motifs. Any of the designs may be used to advantage to decorate items of household furnishings, linens or accessories, either by working directly from the colour pictures or by working from the charts in this section.

The background grid of lines on the charts represents threads of fabric and if you wish to reproduce the design exactly as the colour picture, evenweave fabric with the same number of threads must be used. It is therefore advisable to check the thread count carefully before starting, as a different fabric will alter the finished size of the motif.

To check the thread count, pencil a 2.5cm (1in) square on the coloured picture and then count the number of warp or weft threads in the area. If the design is charted in this section you will be able to count the number of grid lines behind the area of design you have marked on the picture.

Understanding charts

Some charts, such as the Algerian Corner motif on the opposite page show a section of the design and if the design were required to be repeated as a border, this is done by repeating the arrangement of stitches as given.

Other charts, such as that for the Chessboard motif, page 101, give just over a quarter of the design. The large black arrows indicate the centre and, from this, you are able to repeat the quarter section given to work the entire embroidery design.

When working with this type of chart, decide the position of the motif on the fabric and, by counting warp and weft threads, mark the centre of the area with lines of basting threads to coincide with the black arrows on the chart.

The heaver lines on the background grid represent stitches. To reproduce the stitch, count the number of grid lines it covers, then work the stitch over the same number of fabric threads.

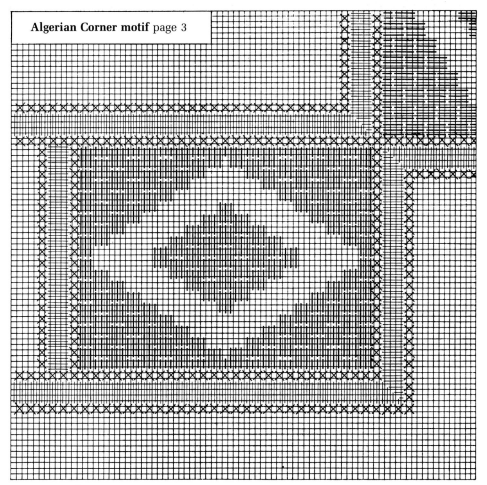

Algerian Corner motif page 3

99

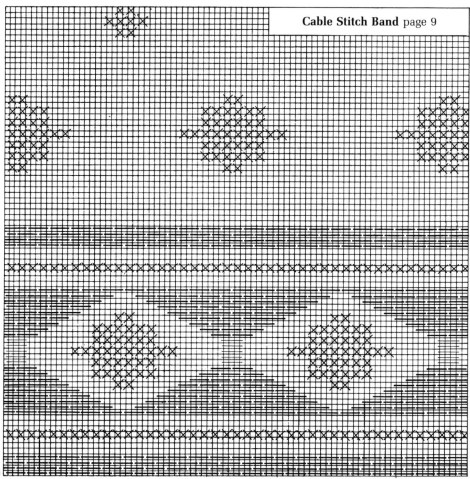

100

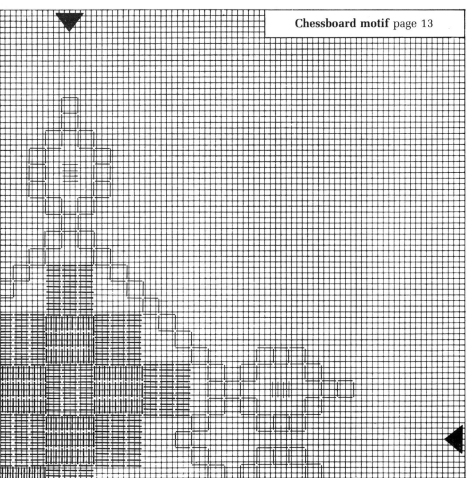

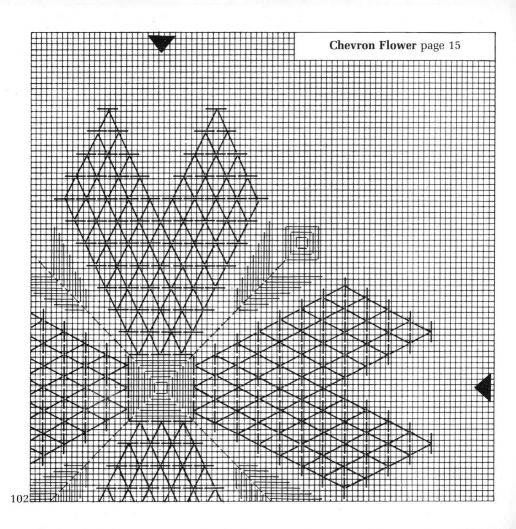

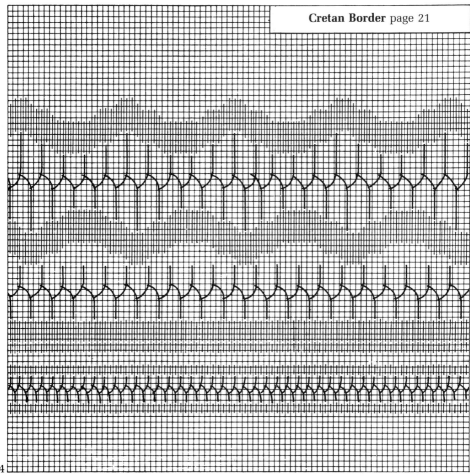

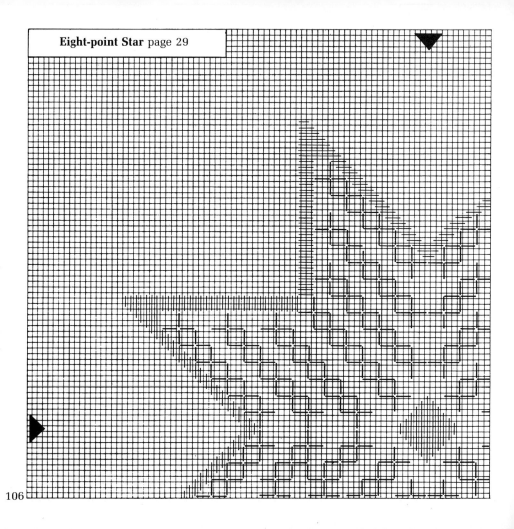

106

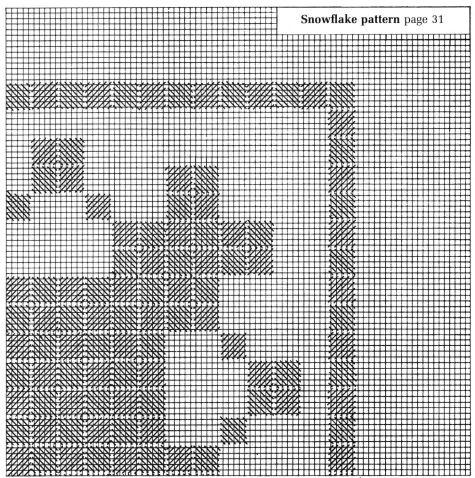

Snowflake pattern page 31

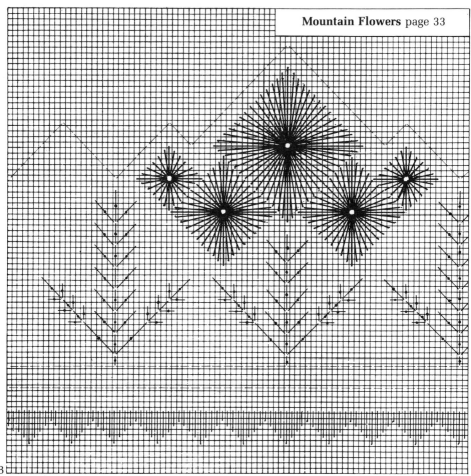

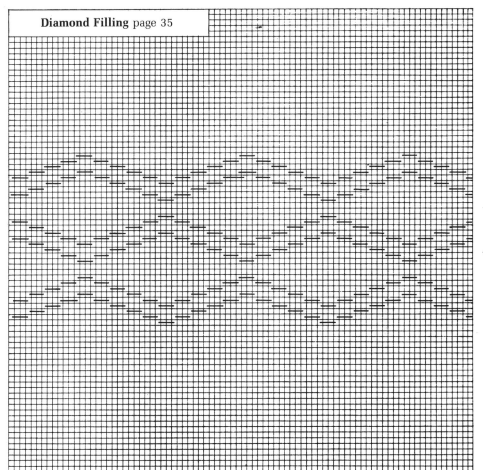

Diamond Filling page 35

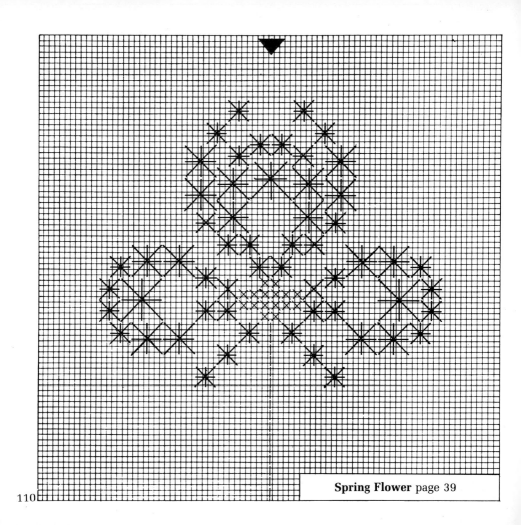

Spring Flower page 39

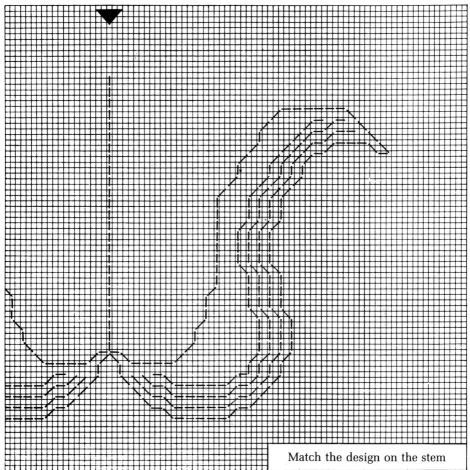

Match the design on the stem

111

Geometric motif page 43

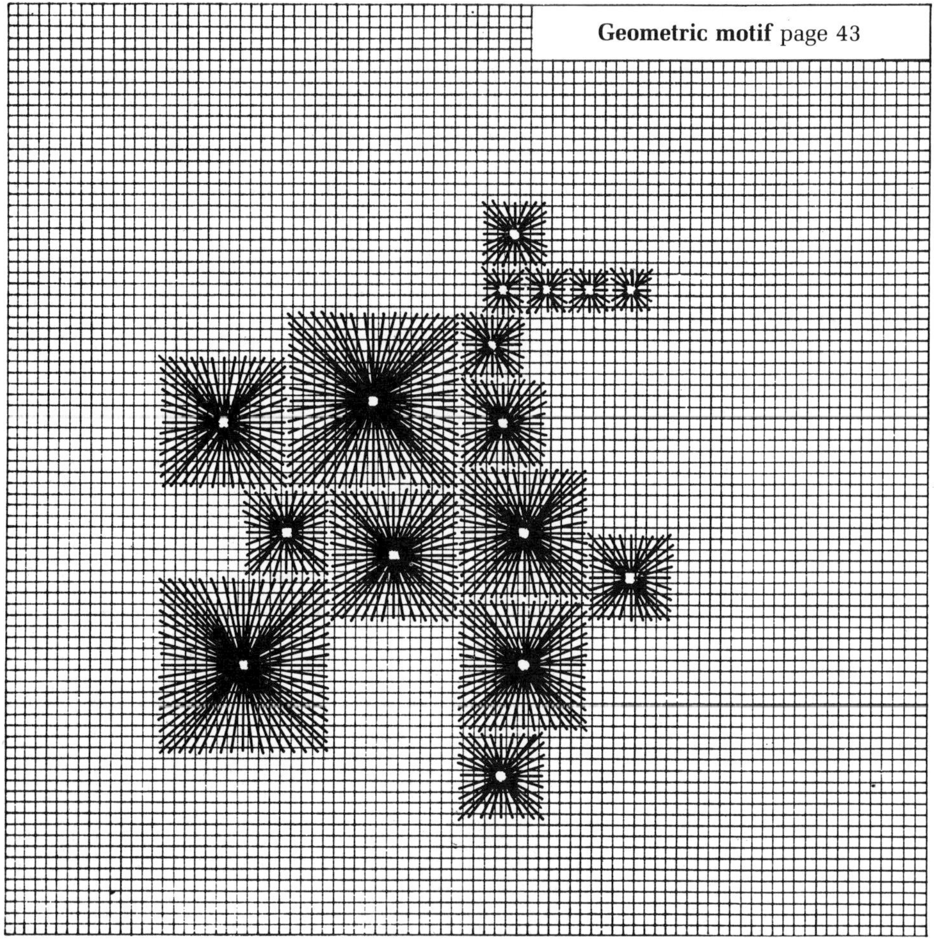

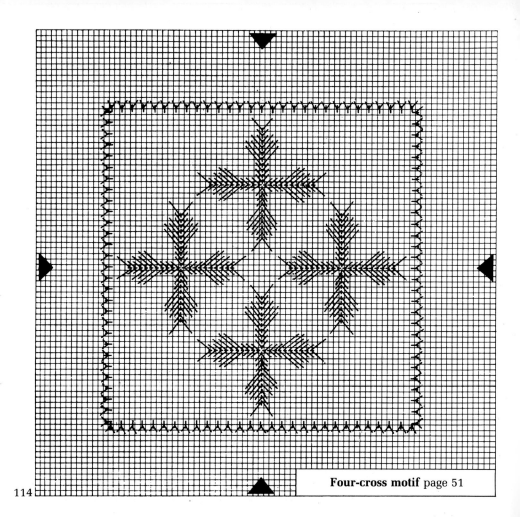

Four-cross motif page 51

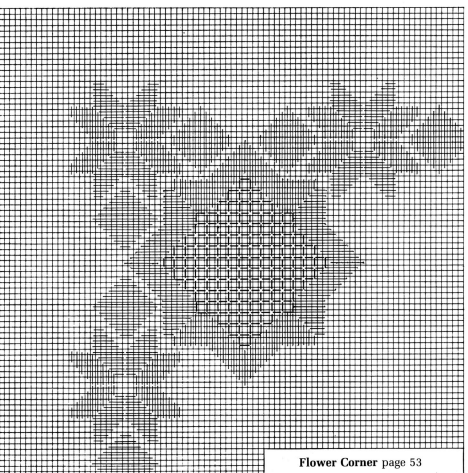

Flower Corner page 53

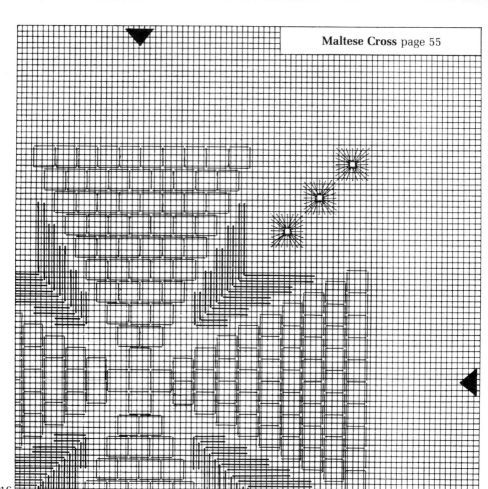

Square on Square page 59

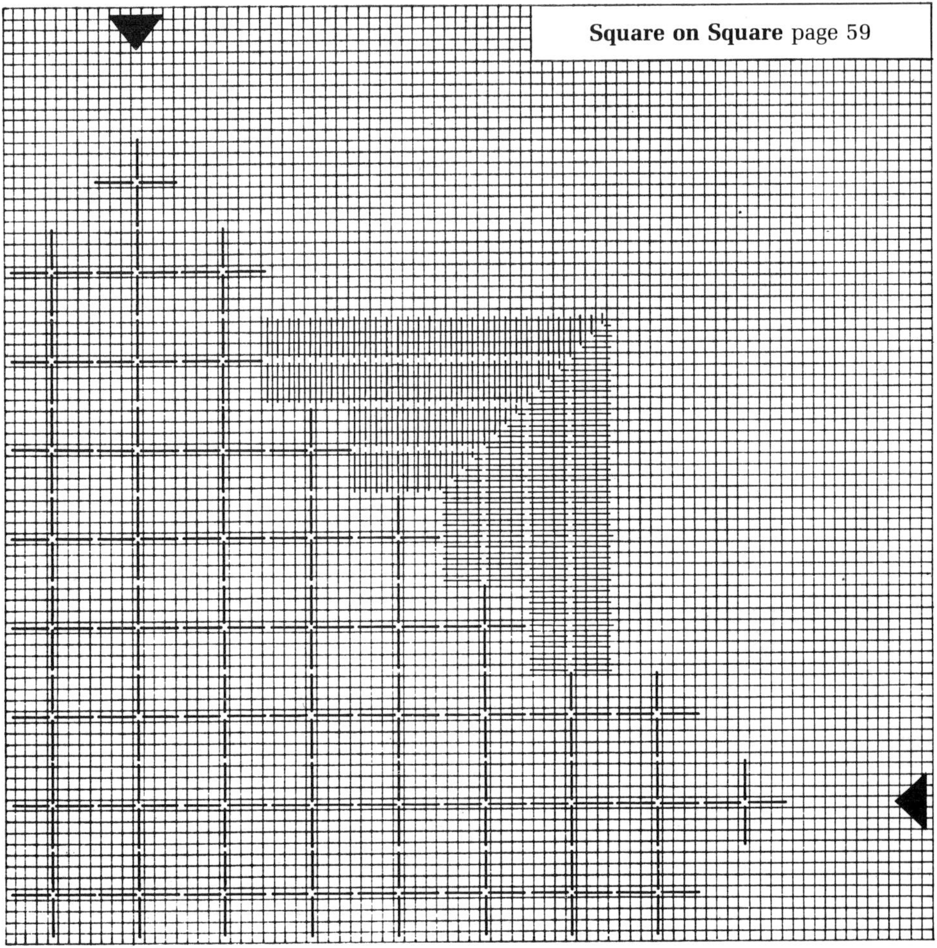

Hedebo edged corner page 61

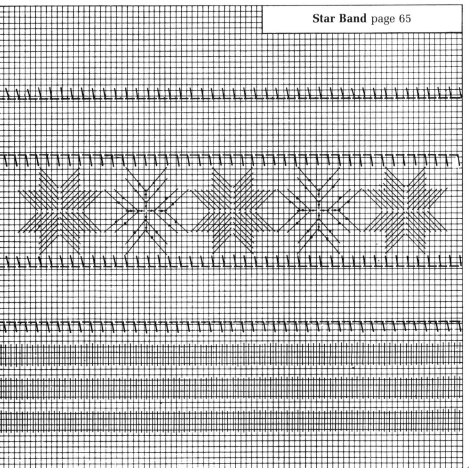

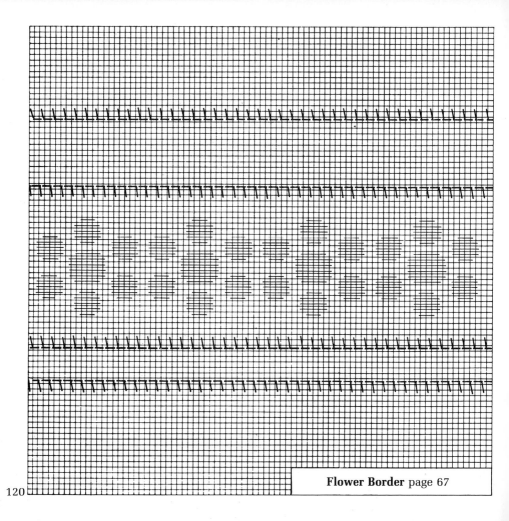

Flower Border page 67

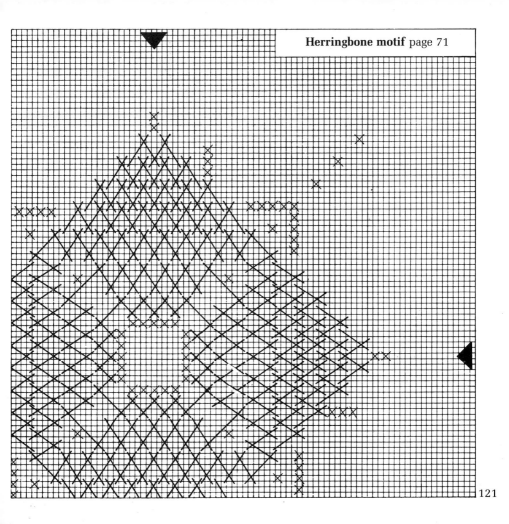

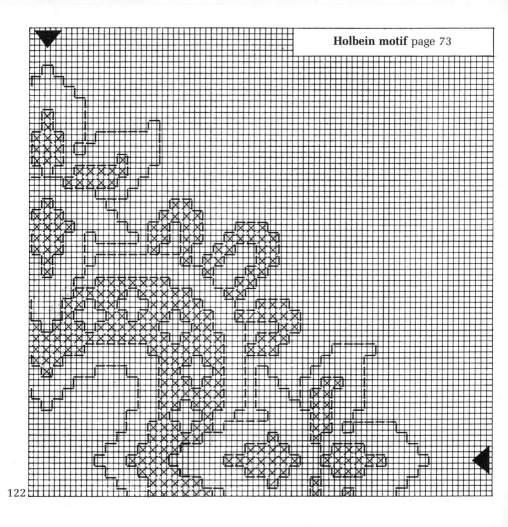

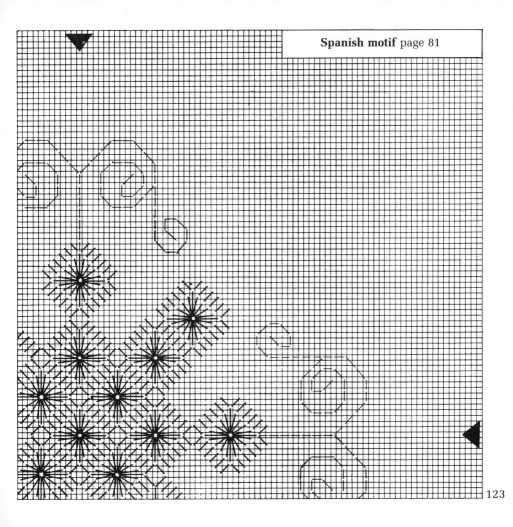

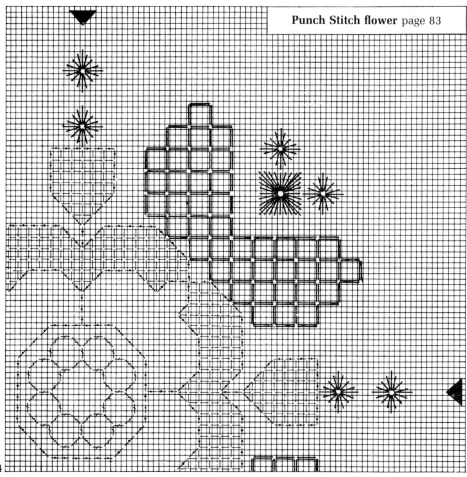

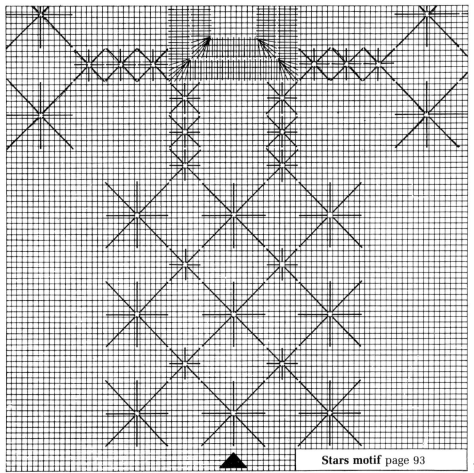

Stars motif page 93

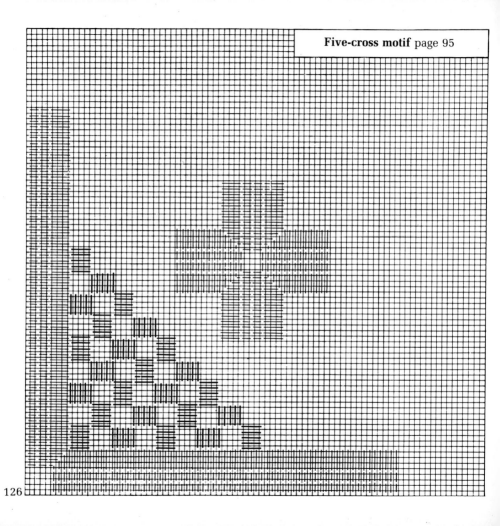

Wave Stitch motif page 96

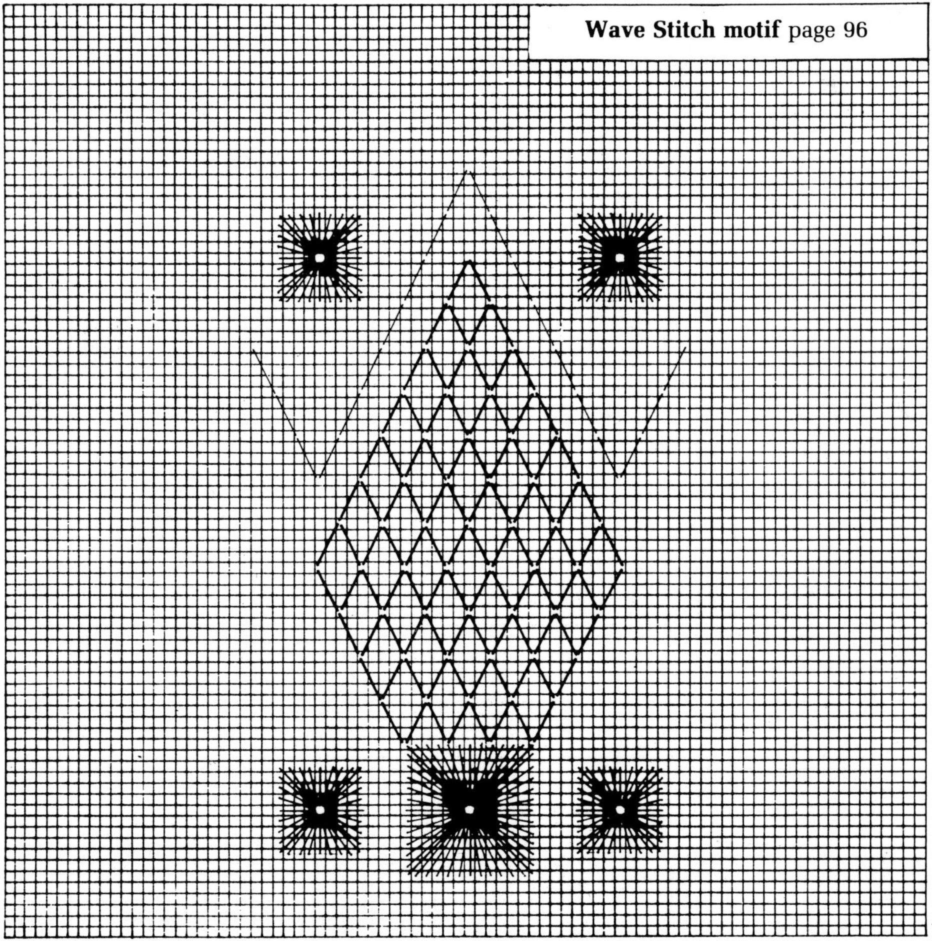

Thread, Needle and Fabric Guide

Fabric	Anchor Embroidery threads	Strand thickness	Milward International Range Needle sizes
			Tapestry Needles (rounded points)
			No. Strand thickness
Fine evenweave fabric	Stranded Cotton Pearl Cotton No. 8, 5 Coton à Broder No. 16	1–6	1 and 2 strands
			24 } 3 strands, Coton à Broder No. 16
Medium weight evenweave fabric, medium mesh canvas, etc.	Stranded Cotton Pearl Cotton No. 8, 5 Coton à Broder No. 16 Tapisserie Wool	3,4 or 6	4 strands, Pearl Cotton No. 8
			20 6 strands, Pearl Cotton No. 5
			18 Soft Embroidery, Tapisserie Wool
Coarse or heavy evenweave fabric, heavy mesh canvas, etc.	Stranded Cotton Pearl Cotton No. 5 Soft Embroidery Tapisserie Wool	4 or 6	
Medium weight square weave canvas	Stranded Cotton Pearl Cotton No. 5 Soft Embroidery Tapisserie Wool	3, 4 or 6	No. Strand thickness 20 6 strands, Pearl Cotton No. 5 18 Soft Embroidery, Tapisserie Wool
Heavy square weave canvas	Stranded Cotton Soft Embroidery Tapisserie Wool	6	

Harlow, Eve
  The new Anchor book of Counted thread embroidery stitches.
  1. Embroidery   I. Title
  746.44′042   TT770
  ISBN 0-7153 8862-2

First published 1987
Reprinted 1987, 1989, 1990, 1991, 1993, 1995
© Text: David & Charles plc 1987
© Illustrations by Jill Shipley J. & P. Coats (UK) Ltd

Phototypeset by Typesetters (Birmingham) Ltd, Smethwick, West Midlands and printed by New Interlitho, Milan, Italy for David & Charles plc
Brunel House   Newton Abbot   Devon